Dramas with a Message

VOLUME FOUR

Books by Doug Fagerstrom

Baker Handbook of Single Adult Ministry (gen. ed.)

Counseling Single Adults (gen. ed.)

Dramas with a Message—Volume One

Dramas with a Message—Volume Two

Dramas with a Message—Volume Three

Dramas with a Message—Volume Four

Dramas with a Message—Volume Five

The Lonely Pew (with Jim Carlson)

Single Adult Ministry, the Second Step (gen. ed.)

Single to God (gen. ed.)

Single to Single (gen. ed.)

Singles Ministries Handbook (gen. ed.)

Worship and Drama Library, volume 15

Dramas with a Message

21 Reproducible Dramatic Sketches for the Local Church

VOLUME FOUR

DOUG FAGERSTROM

Kregel Publications

Dramas with a Message: 21 Reproducible Dramatic Sketches for the Local Church—Volume Four

Published by Kregel Publications, a division of Kregel, Inc., P.O. Box 2607, Grand Rapids, MI 49501. Kregel Publications provides trusted, biblical publications for Christian growth and service. Your comments and suggestions are valued.

Book design: Kevin Ingram

Library of Congress Cataloging-in-Publication Data
Fagerstrom, Douglas L.
Dramas with a message: 21 reproducible dramatic sketches for the local church—volume four / Doug Fagerstrom.
p. cm.
1. Drama in public worship. 2. Drama in Christian education. 3. Christian drama, American. I. Title.
BV289F34 1999 246′.72—dc21 99-43099
CIP

ISBN 0-8254-2581-6 (v. 1)
ISBN 0-8254-2582-4 (v. 2)
ISBN 0-8254-2583-2 (v. 3)
ISBN 0-8254-2586-7 (v. 4)
ISBN 0-8254-2587-5 (v. 5)

Printed in the United States of America
03 04 05 06 07 / 5 4 3 2 1

A Note to the Drama Director

Dramas with a Message is designed for the worship service or special program in local churches or ministries. Sketches are short—about five to seven minutes in length. Stage setup is simple, often needing only a chair, table, or hand props, and you are permitted to photocopy as many scripts as you need. Actors can be inexperienced, since the characters and lines come out of everyday events.

Some sketches are comical (although that is not their primary purpose), some are serious, and some have an ending that will surprise the audience. All of them carry simple themes. They are not complicated with hidden messages or deep theological truths. While the dramas can stand alone, they often work better as illustrations in a service or program. Not every sketch attempts to deliver an entire message. Some leave the audience "hanging" and in need of a speaker to complete the point. You, the director, will determine how best to fit a sketch into its context.

Know your audience. Know the message for the program. Know your actors. Select the right sketch—and then, have fun! Enjoy the sketches. Build a team of actors and support staff who will value being part of a ministry that delivers biblical principles and truths in an entertaining way.

Blessings as you share the message of Good News through these dramas.

Doug Fagerstrom

Acknowledgments

These sketch volumes are dedicated to the faithful actors and actresses at Calvary Church who volunteer their time and talent and have graciously performed these sketches at the "Saturday Night" ministry, each and every week.

Contents

1

He Hit My Car!

Theme

When other people hurt us, the first response is to get revenge, to get even. We soon discover, however, that revenge is never enough. God says to love our enemies and pray for those who persecute us. And that is tough, as we will see in this sketch.

Characters

CLAYTON: Everyman, who responds to everything in life with a tough macho-man mind-set. He is dressed casually—boots, winter jacket, gloves, and so forth.

DWIGHT: Clayton's neighbor. He has a much softer attitude toward life's circumstances than Clayton. He is also dressed casually in a winter coat.

Setting

An empty stage creates an outdoor setting as Clayton shovels the snow off his walk/driveway. Dwight comes by to return the rake he had borrowed about three months prior.

Clayton enters, carrying a snow shovel, and begins the motions of shoveling show, grumbling the entire time. Momentarily, Dwight walks over to Clayton, carrying a leaf rake.

DWIGHT: *[trying to be friendly]* Whoa, slow down there, neighbor. You could hurt yourself.

CLAYTON: *[upset, and sarcastic]* And you could give me a hand . . . neighbor.

DWIGHT: *[casually]* Maybe next time. . . . Actually I just wanted to return the rake I borrowed in the fall.

CLAYTON: *[sarcasm continues]* As in three months ago in the fall?

DWIGHT: *[a bit sheepish]* Well . . . I guess it was. . . . Sorry, Clayton.

CLAYTON: *[serious]* Dwight, tell me why people never keep their promises?

DWIGHT: *[defensive]* Hey, you never told me when you needed the rake back.

CLAYTON: I'm not talking about that stupid rake. In fact, you can keep that piece of junk.

DWIGHT: *[naively]* Thanks! Then what are you talking about?

CLAYTON: *[definitive]* Charlie!

DWIGHT: *[curious]* Charlie?

CLAYTON: Yes, Charlie Jacobson.

DWIGHT: *[more curious]* What about Charlie Jacobson?

CLAYTON: *[upset, but restrained]* He ran into my car . . . and at church of all places.

DWIGHT: *[slow and deliberate]* Ah . . . your . . .

CLAYTON: *[finishes each sentence, with angry tone]* New car.

DWIGHT: The one . . .

CLAYTON: *[upset]* I ordered and waited three months to get it from the dealer.

DWIGHT: With all that . . .

CLAYTON: *[loud]* Special paint color that no one can match.

DWIGHT: So, what did Charlie say?

CLAYTON: "Sorry, man . . . I didn't see you coming around the snow bank."

DWIGHT: *[being realistic . . . trying to make peace]* Well, that sounds fair to me.

CLAYTON: But he doesn't have any insurance.

DWIGHT: Well, they've been hard up since they had those twin boys. It really set them back.

CLAYTON: Dwight, you're not listening . . . *[emphatic]* new car, special paint, no insurance.

DWIGHT: I heard all that . . . I think.

CLAYTON: Then you're not hearing that this is going to cost me a fortune. *[shrewdly]* Or, I may just have to—

DWIGHT: No . . . don't say it, Clayton.

CLAYTON: Say, what?

DWIGHT: I know what you want to say. . . . I know you, Clayton.

CLAYTON: Sue! . . . There I said it. Does that bother you? . . . Sue, ha, there I said it again. I'm taking that irresponsible man to court. He needs to learn a lesson!

DWIGHT: *[pleading tone]* You'll ruin him . . . and his family. . . . They can't pay you. . . . They don't have anything.

CLAYTON: *[upset, cold, and stoic]* Then he shouldn't be driving a car.

DWIGHT: *[firm, but kind]* Here's your rake, Clayton. I think I'll be going now.

CLAYTON: *[no response, just a disgusted look]*

DWIGHT: *[walks away, stops, contemplates, speaks]* Clayton?

CLAYTON: Yeah, now what?

DWIGHT: *[strong, not satirical nor angry]* Clayton, go get your car fixed and send me the bill.

CLAYTON: *[sarcastic]* So now my neighbor is the Good Samaritan.

DWIGHT: No, not at all. *[pause]* I just care about those little twins . . . and their mom and dad.

[freeze; blackout]

2

The Price of Love

Theme

It is impossible to place a value on human life. But God did. He gave his Son for us to live. In this real life parable, parents are asked to place a value on their broken son in jail. For his mistake (being in the wrong place at the wrong time), it will cost them everything to get him free.

Characters

Mike Donaldson: An American middle-class husband and father. He is asked to give up everything for his son. He is dressed in a sport coat and tie, but his slacks do not match his outfit (not intended to be comic).

Jane Donaldson: Mike's wife. She wears a dress, but shoes and coat obviously do not match. She is embarrassed by Mike's slacks and her own outfit.

William Armstrong: Attorney-at-Law, is tough and bold. Dressed in a suit, he has no sympathy for the Donaldsons' plight and dilemma.

Setting

A desk, desk chair, and two side chairs across from the desk create an attorney's office.

As music plays, Armstrong enters from stage left to take a seat at his desk. The Donaldson's enter stage right as they begin a dialogue with each other outside the office.

Jane: *[embarrassed, almost in tears]* Mike, I'm so ashamed.

Mike: *[consoling his wife]* Jane . . . you need to pull yourself together. We don't have a choice.

Jane: *[concerned]* Are you sure this attorney is any good?

Mike: *[convincing]* He's been recommended by everyone I talked to. We're lucky to get him.

Jane: *[naive]* Well, "junkyard lawyer" just doesn't sound like the best qualifications to me.

Mike: We need someone who's going to be tough.

Jane: *[sighs]* Did you have to wear those slacks with that coat? They don't even match.

MIKE: I'm sorry. . . . Let's just meet this guy and get this over with. *[They move into the office area.]* Hello, are you Mr. Armstrong?

ARMSTRONG: *[only looking up for a moment as he studies his file folder]* Yes, William Armstrong, have a seat. You must be the Donaldsons.

MIKE: *[nervous, trying to break the ice]* I'm Mike and this is Jane . . .

ARMSTRONG: *[straightforward]* I hope you understand we have a big problem.

JANE: *[helpless]* We know that, but everyone says you can help us.

ARMSTRONG: Well, God I am not . . . but right now He can't help you very much, so you're stuck with me.

MIKE: *[desperate tone]* So what do we do? Our son is innocent, you know.

ARMSTRONG: *[skeptical]* According to whom?

JANE: *[strong, defensive]* My boy didn't do any of those things. . . . They're all lies.

ARMSTRONG: Look, Mrs. Donaldson, I don't know your son, but I know that he's in big trouble. And maybe, just maybe, he was in the wrong place at the wrong time. But this isn't going to be easy.

MIKE: So what is it going to take?

ARMSTRONG: The bottom line?

MIKE: *[yielded]* Just give it to us.

ARMSTRONG: A lot money and a lot of time.

JANE: We have lots of time.

MIKE: *[very concerned]* How much money?

ARMSTRONG: What do you have in savings?

MIKE: A few thousand dollars.

ARMSTRONG: Any equity in your home?

MIKE: Oh, maybe $40,000 to $50,000.

JANE: Mike, what's going on here?

ARMSTRONG: I'm sorry, but you need to sell your home, and we need the cash right away if we're going to meet bail and start our initial investigation. And you know this could take us a year.

JANE: *[upset, as if the wind has just been knocked out of her]* Mike, did you know this was going to cost us our home and . . . and everything we have . . . and take a year?

MIKE: *[trying to be firm]* No, Jane, I didn't know. *[to Armstrong]* Look . . . our son did not . . . could not have done anything he's accused of. Can't we just get him acquitted or agree this is just some kind of mistake?

ARMSTRONG: I'm sorry, it's just not that easy. A jury is going to have to decide all of that. I think we have a chance, but there are no shortcuts. So, it's up to you.

MIKE: *[Jane and Mike just look at each other, then to Armstrong.]* I'll have the money for you tomorrow, and I'll take care of the rest. Just tell me how much.

JANE: *[strong and passionate]* Mr. Armstrong, we'll give you everything we have. You just get our son back.

[Music begins to play.]

ARMSTRONG: You really love this kid, don't you?

MIKE: More than you will ever know.

ARMSTRONG: I'll do everything I can.

[Music swells; lights dim; everyone leaves.]

3

Healing, but No Celebration

Theme

Jesus does heal. Every time Jesus heals, it's a miracle. But not everyone celebrates the work of Jesus. As you will see in this "New Testament story," the religious leaders became indignant when a woman with an infirmity is healed on the Sabbath. There is no one to share her joy.

Characters

Larry Sting: Our modern-day talk show host, resembling a popular nighttime host on TV.

Rachael: Our healed woman appears in first-century dress to report her story. She is about thirty-five to forty-five years old.

Setting

A small desk with microphones and two chairs are at stage center.

As the music plays, Larry enters and greets his audience and introduces the show. Music winds down as he begins to speak.

Larry: *[unemotional]* Ladies and gentlemen, welcome to another edition of Larry Sting Live, and tonight we'll be talking to a guest who claims to have been healed by Jesus of Nazareth, an unknown carpenter from a village so small that very few people have even heard of it. So we have an interesting story, but we'll let her tell it. Please welcome Rachael Johnson. *[Music plays to bring Rachel out.]* Rachael, welcome to our show.

Rachael: *[very delighted; music winds down]* Thank you, Larry. It's very good to be here.

Larry: *[skeptical]* Now, we have a report that you used to be crippled with a terrible spinal problem.

Rachael: *[jumps right in with a positive spirit]* Could never straighten up . . . since I was twenty years old.

Larry: That certainly is a long time.

RACHAEL: *[positive spirit continues]* Half of my life. You need to be grateful and learn to thank God it wasn't you.

LARRY: So, Rachael, you walked in here rather straight. . . . You don't appear to have any problems.

RACHAEL: Listen, Larry, I have the best story to tell you, and it's all about Jesus.

LARRY: *[uncomfortable]* Ah, the carpenter from Nazareth?

RACHAEL: Maybe He is a carpenter, but not just a carpenter to me. *[much passion]* He's the healer of broken bodies. Jesus came into the synagogue last week on Saturday afternoon. He called me forward, and that's unheard of in the Synagogue—a man calling on a woman *[voice raises]* on the Sabbath. Why, the ruler of the synagogue has never called on me. *[soft voice]* They just ignore women.

LARRY: *[coy]* I'm beginning to understand—

RACHAEL: *[cuts Larry off]* Anyway, He called me . . . that is, Jesus called me, and said, "Rachael, you are set free from your infirmity." *[leaning forward]* And then He put His hand on me.

LARRY: *[hostily]* He said that and touched you?

RACHAEL: *[not pleased]* You're beginning to sound just like the rest of those guys. *[indignant]* Yes, He said that, and He touched me, and I stood straight up as if I were nineteen years old again!

LARRY: *[not excited, reads from a newspaper]* I understand there's a little controversy with what has happened to you.

RACHAEL: *[unhappy]* That depends on who you talk to.

LARRY: *[factual]* Well, you know that healing on the Sabbath is unlawful.

RACHAEL: That's just what the ruler of the synagogue said. In fact, he and Jesus got into quite an argument . . . over what happened to me!

LARRY: *[enjoying the turn of conversation]* Oh really? Tell me about this "argument."

RACHAEL: No big deal. The ruler said Jesus shouldn't have healed. And Jesus disagreed with . . . something about watering your donkey on the Sabbath.

LARRY: So how do you feel about this?

RACHAEL: To be honest, a little sad.

LARRY: *[pushes back]* Wait a minute, you came in here claiming that Jesus healed you from *[picks up paper]* eighteen years of being crippled, and you're sad. I don't get it.

RACHAEL: I don't expect you to. But I'll tell you what I don't get—my religious leader never prayed for me to be healed. Jesus heals me and no one is there to share my joy. That's what I don't get.

LARRY: Why do you think no one is jumping up and down?

RACHAEL: *[softened]* I'm not sure, Mr. Larry. It really hurts when the best thing that ever happened to me gets criticized and put down. I just don't get it.

LARRY: *[reporting to the audience]* Well, folks, this is quite a report. An apparent healing on the Sabbath and a major argument in the synagogue. I'm not sure where all of this is leading.

RACHAEL: Apparent healing? I don't think so. Where is this leading? Well, it's led me to love Jesus . . . and the Messiah.

LARRY: But if this Jesus really healed you as you've said, then why doesn't everyone flock to see Him and get healed?

RACHAEL: I don't know, Mr. Larry. Like I said, I just don't get it. I just don't get it.

[freeze; blackout]

4 Cain, Where's Abel?

Theme

Murder has been around for a long time—since Adam and Eve's two sons learned what jealousy, envy, hatred, and self-preservation are all about. The story is simple—and very sad. And it continues in the lives of people today.

Characters

Cain: Dressed in an early- or current-century farmer's outfit.

Voice: The voice of God offstage is very real and nonjudging.

Setting

A simple rock or bench or a place for Cain to sit.

Music plays a very simple tune or rhythm as Cain enters from backstage, "looking for a place to hide." He finally ends upstage center, looking around, scared, and a bit cold in a semi-fetal position.

Voice: *[kind, but strong voice]* Cain, is that you? *[Cain looks around and does not respond out of his fear]* Where are you, Cain? *[Cain looks for a place to run, but realizes it is hopeless]* Cain?

Cain: *[pretends that nothing is wrong and sounds cordial]* Oh . . . ah, hi, God . . . how Ya doing?

Voice: Actually, I wanted to ask *you* that question?

Cain: *[tries to be upbeat]* Well, the answer is 'great!' Hey, couldn't be better. *[looks around with several "guilty" expressions]*

Voice: Really? You don't look so good.

Cain: *[nervous, scrambling for every line]* Ah . . . tough day, God . . . yeah, tough day . . . plowing those fields, raising those crops. . . . A lot of hard work. . . . That's it . . . I'm tired . . . from all of the hard work. . . . So, I'll just lay down . . . right here and take a nap. *[starts to do just that]*

Voice: You don't look tired; you look a little down.

CAIN: *[more nervous]* Down? You got it, God. . . . I am down . . . Oh . . . way down . . . in the depths . . . right at the bottom of down. . . . In fact, place me below down, God . . . really . . . really down.

VOICE: How did you get there . . . so far down?

CAIN: *[tries to sound logical]* I'm . . . not real sure, God. . . . I guess I just found myself there.

VOICE: *[trying to lead Cain]* No reason at all?

CAIN: *[curious]* Why are You asking all of these questions, God?

VOICE: I guess I just wanted to talk with you and find out from you how your day has gone.

CAIN: *[strong]* Look, God, can we just chalk this day up to experience and . . . you know, forget about this day and move on to another day . . . like . . . tomorrow?

VOICE: I don't think so. . . . What is that tucked in your belt, Cain?

CAIN: *[Cain pulls out a ram's horn.]* A ram's horn . . . you know for blowing notes. . . . You want to hear?

VOICE: No, let's just say that I'm not into music right now. So, where is your brother, Abel?

CAIN: *[tries to make it short and sweet]* I don't know.

VOICE: Have you seen him recently?

CAIN: *[more deliberate]* I don't know.

VOICE: I thought the two of you went out into the field this afternoon.

CAIN: *[angry]* Well, if You saw that, then maybe You know where he is.

VOICE: You don't need to get upset—I was just asking.

CAIN: *[logical]* Look, am I my brother's keeper?

VOICE: Cain *[short pause]* what have you done? *[long pause]* I'm waiting for your reply.

CAIN: Look, God, it just isn't fair. I couldn't impress You like Abel did . . . and . . .

VOICE: *[short pause]* And?

CAIN: And I struck him with this. *[holds up ram's horn, or rod, clenched teeth]* He made me so mad. *[stunned]* Then . . . he wouldn't get up . . . he wouldn't get up.

VOICE: Cain, you know I can't turn my back on this.

CAIN: What are You going to do? *[As if he has a good idea, he holds up the ram's horn.]* Here, God, hit me with this. . . . It's only fair. *[Cain closes eyes as he shrinks with his arm extended high with the horn.]*

VOICE: Put the horn down, Cain. *[Music begins, lights start going down.]* But you must leave this land, wander in another land, and work harder than you've ever worked. You'll never forget this day as long as you live. *[Lights are out at this point.]* However, . . . I will protect you . . . only because I love you.

CAIN: *[Audience can only hear a passionate but weak plea.]* God . . . . Abel, I'm so sorry.

[Music increases as Cain exits the platform.]

5

The Bible Tells Me So

Theme

Many people question the truth of the Bible, and some consider the stories in the Bible as myths. Question: Does it take the mind and discipline of a scholar to believe the truth of God's Word? The answer from this sketch is "no" as two children learn to trust God's Word as true.

Characters

ANGIE: A little girl about six or seven years old. Pigtails, ribbons, and bright-colored clothes let everyone know she is a child. She is a happy little girl.

BRENDA: Angie's good friend. She is also six or seven years old, also bright and cheerful. She has big freckles, a ponytail, and wears bright colors.

Setting

A bench or couch allows the girls to be sitting next to each other. Each girl has a book and bag lunch. A stuffed dog or small doll is optional.

Director's Note: This sketch can be fun when played by adults.

Angie enters as the music is playing a children's theme song and finds her place on the bench. She takes a drink box out of her lunch sack, takes a swallow, and begins to read the large hardback book that she has carried under her arm. As the music continues to play, Brenda skips in, finds her seat next to Angie, digs immediately into her lunch bag, pulls out a peanut butter sandwich, and starts eating. Brenda soon notices Angie, smiles, and leans over to see what book she's reading. Music stops as Brenda starts to speak. Both girls are kind and sweet to each other.

BRENDA: *[speaks with her mouth full; barely understandable]* Hi, Angie.

ANGIE: Hi, Brenda!

BRENDA: *[not clear]* Whatcha doing?

ANGIE: *[confused]* What did ya say?

BRENDA: *[still not clear]* Whatcha doing?

ANGIE: Brenda, I can't understand you with peanut butter in your mouth.

BRENDA: *[points at book, makes a huge swallow]* What are you doing?

ANGIE: I'm reading my book.

BRENDA: What book are you reading?

ANGIE: I'm reading my Bible story book that my gramma and grampa gave me.

BRENDA: *[inquisitive]* What's the story about?

ANGIE: *[simply reports the facts]* It's about Noah and a big boat.

BRENDA: I don't think I ever heard that story?

ANGIE: Well . . . it's really a good story.

BRENDA: Well . . . where did Noah go with his big boat?

ANGIE: Well . . . he didn't go anywhere with his big boat.

BRENDA: Then why did he have a big boat?

ANGIE: To give the animals a ride.

BRENDA: What animals? Did he take a dog in his boat, 'cause my dad said that my dog can't go in his fissin boat any more 'cause he is too noisy . . . and he scares away all the fiss.

ANGIE: The story says that Noah took all the animals in the boat.

BRENDA: That was nice of Noah. . . . How long was the ride?

ANGIE: The story says it was for forty days and forty nights.

BRENDA: That's a long time to go nowhere. That's longer than the ride to my gramma's house, and my dad has to stop at the Standard gas station in Indiana if I drink all of my Pepsi. Then what did Noah do?

ANGIE: He got out of the boat.

BRENDA: *[as sweet as ever]* So . . . Noah took all the animals on a forty-day boat ride, didn't go nowhere, and just got out of the boat?

ANGIE: Uh huh.

BRENDA: Angie?

ANGIE: Yeah?

BRENDA: That's kind of a dumb story.

ANGIE: Why?

BRENDA: 'Cause it's not true.

ANGIE: But it is true, Brenda.

BRENDA: Then it's really hard to believe . . . or that guy Noah was kinda dumb.

ANGIE: But my grampa said, "All the Bible stories are true."

BRENDA: How does your grampa know? Did he talk to Mr. Noah?

ANGIE: Maybe! Maybe not!

BRENDA: Well, if he didn't talk to Mr. Noah, then how come he believes in that funny story about a man in a boat with animals going nowhere.

ANGIE: 'Cause God wrote it.

BRENDA: How does he know that? Did God tell that to your grampa?

ANGIE: Uh huh.

BRENDA: Really? When did He tell him that?

ANGIE: Last summer when it rained on my grampa's farm.

BRENDA: That's when God told your grampa He wrote the Bible?

ANGIE: No, that's when my grampa talked to God, and God came through with rain for my grampa. And grampa said, "God is true and His Word is true, too."

BRENDA: Wow! Are there any more God stories?

ANGIE: Uh huh.

BRENDA: If you tell me one, I'll give you the other half of my peanut butter sandwich.

ANGIE: OK. *[Takes sandwich and a big bite; begins to mumble through a story as the girls squeeze together and read the storybook; lights go dim and the music comes up over the mumbling.]*

[fadeout; exit during music]

6

Hello, God? Life Is Tough!

Theme

We all go through tough days. When we do, God often receives the blame when things go wrong, or He is questioned why life does not go the way we would like it to go. In the following three sketches people go through tough days, and we see their response.

Characters

Martha: Everywoman, who has just received news that she has lost her job. Dress is casual.

Jennifer: A young woman who discovers that a broken engagement is not the end of the world. Dress is very casual.

Sally: Believes that the news of cancer is God's way of punishing her for a past life of sin and disobedience. Dress is casual.

Messenger: Dressed in white from head to toe and helps the above three connect with God.

Voice: Represents the voice of God by speaking and reading Scripture as answers to their tough questions.

Setting

Scene 1: At stage right Martha is seated in a chair going through the mail.

Scene 2: At stage center Jennifer is seated in a chair talking on the phone to her boyfriend.

Scene 3: At stage left Sally sits in a waiting room chair, just outside of a doctor's office.

Everyone above enters, takes their places onstage, and freezes. Each comes to action at the beginning of each personal speech, and then returns to a freeze position after speaking.

SCENE 1

Going through mail and tossing all mail on the floor while Messenger with cell phone is watching every move from behind her chair.

Martha: *[casual]* Junk mail; You won ten million dollars . . . sure, Ed McMann; new credit card at seven-point-nine percent; new credit card at eight-point-nine percent; new credit card at eighteen-point-nine percent; Builders Square; light bill; gas bill; phone bill; Taco Bell coupons; *[puts in pocket]* vote for . . . Ah, here it is, my vacation check. . . . Oh, it's going to be tough going back to work on Monday. *[sits back as if dreaming]* This has been the best two weeks off to paint, wallpaper the porch, play tennis, and do a little extra shopping. . . . But I can't have fun every day. *[opens envelope and begins to read; short pause]* We will no longer be needing your services as the company is downsizing. *[repeats loudly]* Downsizing? *[mumbles . . . getting excited and louder]* And you need to clean out your desk by Monday, *[read a calendar date]* and return your key for the fifth floor washroom. *[dismayed]* I can't believe it. I've worked for Harold Caseworth and Company for nineteen years and just before I'm fully vested in the twenty-year program, they can me. I simply can't— *[looks up to heaven]* And to think I trusted You to come through. Great, now how am I going to take care of my family? How am I, as a single parent, supposed to send my son Jim to college? Hello? Is anyone up there?

MESSENGER: Ah, excuse me. *[Martha jumps.]*

MARTHA: *[frightened]* Whoa! Who are you? What are you doing in my home? Did Caseworth send you to check up on me?

MESSENGER: *[soft and kind]* No . . . just call me a friend. I couldn't help but overhear that you were praying.

MARTHA: *[embarrassed]* Well . . . not really. You know, I was just . . . expressing myself *[upset]* to you-know-who.

MESSENGER: Oh, yes, I know who He is . . . rather well. . . . In fact, would you like to talk to Him more directly? *[offers Martha a cell phone]*

MARTHA: Okay, what's the catch?

MESSENGER: No catch, just press the gold button. Here. *[hands off cell phone]*

MARTHA: *[Martha takes cell phone, presses button, says . . .]* Hello? Hello?

VOICE: *[strong, yet kind voice]* Hello, Martha, how are you?

MARTHA: *[upset]* How am I? As if You don't know.

VOICE: I know, I just wanted you to tell Me.

MARTHA: I just lost my job and You want to ask questions?

VOICE: Would you like Me to say more?

MARTHA: You better believe it . . . and a few lightning bolts on Harold Caseworth and Company would be great.

VOICE: Sorry, Martha, no lightning. But I do have a message for you: "You know the plans I have for you, not to harm you, but to give you a future and a hope."

MARTHA: *[shocked]* That's it?

VOICE: For now, that's probably enough.

MARTHA: *[pleading]* Come on, I need some more.

VOICE: Okay, I still love you, more than anything. *[Martha remains frozen; hands the phone to Messenger.]*

MARTHA: Here. I'm done with this. *[sits]*

MESSENGER: What did He say?

MARTHA: Nothing. Nothing that can *[picks up the bills and throws a few across the stage and holds the rest]* help with these.

[freeze; blackout]

SCENE 2

Light comes up on Jennifer, who is talking on the phone.

JENNIFER: *[pleading and hopeful]* Tom, please don't tell me it's over. We have so much in common. We even like the same kind of pizza, and I promise I'll never take my dog "Killer" on another date. Please, Tom, don't break up with me . . . please. *[pause, becomes very downcast]* Yes, I understand . . . right, Tom . . . fine. . . . Sure you can come over and get some of your things in an hour. . . . The door will be open. *[hangs up and speaks with anger]* But I won't be here. Men! I can't believe it. Life is so unfair. If I was only three inches taller, twenty pounds lighter, three years older, and funnier, I wouldn't be in this pain and mess.

MESSENGER: Excuse me but you are not a mess.

JENNIFER: *[not startled and not amused]* And what would you know about that?

MESSENGER: *[clear and concise]* You are not a mess!

JENNIFER: *[oblivious that this is a stranger]* Thank you, Sigmund Freud, but you do not know me.

MESSENGER: Maybe not as well as I should, but would you like to talk to someone who does? *[offers cell phone]*

JENNIFER: *[grabs phone with a ray of hope]* Tom, is that you?

VOICE: Sorry, this is not Tom.

JENNIFER: Who is this?

VOICE: It's been awhile since we talked.

JENNIFER: *[realizes, looks up]* Whoa . . . hey, is this thing with Tom some kind of punishment? Look, just tell me where I blew it; I'll make it right with my parents, and sister, and You, of course, but just give me Tom back. *[convinced she has said the right things]* Okay, deal?

VOICE: You won't be alone. I'll be with you forever and forever! *[Jennifer looks strangely at the phone.]*

MESSENGER: What did He say?

JENNIFER: Nothing . . . absolutely nothing. . . . He just doesn't get it. . . . He just doesn't understand how lonely I'm going to be without Tom. *[hands phone back]* Here, I don't think this works very well.

[freeze; blackout]

SCENE 3

The lights comes up on Sally, seated in her chair, as she looks at a piece of paper.

SALLY: *[stunned]* I can't believe it. Cancer. Cancer. I thought that was for other people . . . not me. *[looks up toward heaven]* Why me? Was I that bad? Did You not like everything I did for You? *[intensely]* Don't you want me to have that vacation of a lifetime our family was planning next month?

MESSENGER: *[approaches]* Excuse me. *[Sally slowly looks at Messenger.]* Would you like to speak more directly to God? *[hands cell phone to Sally]*

SALLY: Sure . . . but what good would that do now? Isn't it too late? *[brings phone up to ear]* You heard me, didn't You? Go ahead, tell me it's too late for me. I mean . . . I might as well have bad news from You today too. *[trying to be tough]* I can take it . . . talk to me!

VOICE: Sally, I know what pain and death is all about.

SALLY: *[surprised]* How would You know that?

VOICE: I loved you so much that I gave my only Son to die a really rough death for you, so that after your cancer you can have life, and have the greatest life forever . . . here with Me.

SALLY: Does that mean You're going to heal me?

VOICE: Eventually I will, Sally. Eventually I will.

MESSENGER: Excuse me, but what did He say?

SALLY: He said it's going to be all right, and I sure hope He's right.

[freeze; blackout]

7

Does God Cause Mistakes?

Theme

Everyone makes mistakes—the errors, blunders, and inaccuracies of life that we cannot escape. When we "blow it" we tend to look for a cover-up or a place to lay blame or find fault. Our characters in this sketch have become experts at laying the blame on others—including God.

Characters

BEN BLOOPER: Represents everyman with every excuse in the book. He is dressed in business attire.

BETTY BLOOPER: Ben's wife, who has learned well from Ben to blame everyone for everything. She's dressed in casual clothes, wearing an apron.

Setting

Scene 1: Stage right is Ben's office, complete with a phone; stage left is Betty's kitchen, with all of the items and appliances needed to make a cake.

Scene 2: The Bloopers' kitchen.

Director's Note: This sketch can be done in two scenes, or the two scenes can flow together.

SCENE 1

While background music plays, Ben enters and sits to work at his desk, drinking his cup of coffee. Betty enters and works on baking a cake. Note: When one is speaking, the other is acting out their role in mime.

BEN: *[spills coffee on himself. Director's note: you need a real spill that will leave a real stain on Ben's white shirt. He yells and responds in anger.]* Good grief, why can't they make a cup like they used to? How is anyone supposed to drink out of this stupid thing without burning themselves?

BETTY: *[cracks egg into bowl, notices a few pieces of shell have fallen into the bowl, responds, upset and whiny]* I can't believe this, eggshells in my cake mix. That is the last time I buy eggs from Sid's D and X Market. They can't even make an egg to crack open like they used to. What's this world coming to?

BEN: *[phone ringing, responds angrily]* Of course . . . the phone always rings right in the middle of my busiest time of the day. Alexander Graham Bell should have been locked up for inventing this stupid thing. His handiwork has ruined my work. *[change of voice to kindness]* Hello, customer service—how can I help you?

BETTY: *[reading cookbook]* How am I supposed to measure three-eighths of a cup of shortening when my cheap husband doesn't buy me measuring cups, especially after I put them on my Christmas list. . . . You'd think that Betty Crocker and Duncan Hines would understand how cheap husbands are and write simpler instructions to make a simple cake. Those people should have been shot.

BEN: *[on the phone, trying hard to keep from losing his cool]* What do you mean, the fan doesn't work? *[short pause]* Did you try the switch? *[short pause]* Did you plug it in? *[getting louder and angry]* Did you read the instructions? Did you use it between 10:00 and 11:30 in the morning? *[pause]* How should I know what's wrong with your stupid oven? Is my last name Amana? Are my initials GE? *[extremely cynical]* No, lady, no. I'm sick and tired of people who don't know what they're doing . . . calling me and blaming me for their stupid idiotic mistakes. We sell stoves. We don't fix them and we don't break them; that's your job. Call Ken More, maybe he can help you! *[slams phone down]*

BETTY: *[loud and angry]* What? Vanilla? Nobody told me this cake was going to require vanilla. Why can't they put these ingredients in bold print for every American to see? They just throw in these last-minute surprises right in the middle of baking their dumb cake.

BEN: Great . . . now my pen is out of ink. Why can't they make a pen that doesn't run out of ink?

BETTY: Great . . . now my mixer won't work. Why can't they make a mixer that can get through just one cake?

BEN: Good night, look what time it is!

BETTY: Good night, look what time it is!

BEN: How am I supposed to get . . .

BETTY: . . . anything done around here . . .

BEN/BETTY: *[unison]* when everybody messes me up!

SCENE 2

BEN: *[comes to the kitchen, looking out-of-sorts]* Betty, I'm home.

BETTY: Well it's about time . . . one hour late.

BEN: *[special complaining voice]* Hey, it's not my fault. Blame _________ *[says name of a popular local highway]* for building a lousy freeway. And how come dinner isn't ready?

BETTY: *[mimics his tone of voice]* Hey, it's not my fault. Blame the galloping gourmet for writing lousy baking instructions. So where's the milk?

BEN: *[obviously forgot the milk]* Ah, the milk . . . right . . . out of milk. D & X was out of milk. Besides, if you had written me a note maybe I could have gotten your milk.

BETTY: *[goes over to the door and picks up paper that says in large print "BEN, GET MILK," very cynical]* You mean like this one that was on the door on your way out this morning?

BEN: Oh yeah, blame me. . . . It's all my fault for not seeing your note in a place that's . . . that's too obvious—yeah, too obvious. Anyone would have missed that note.

BETTY: *[angry]* You can never be wrong, can you?

BEN: *[cynical]* And you're the perfect one.

BETTY: And what's that on your shirt? *[loud]* That was clean this morning.

BEN: Look, Betty, I've had just about enough of you *[phone rings]* blaming me for—

BETTY: Hello, house of perfection where Ben never does anything wrong. Oh, hi, honey. How's my little grandbaby coming along? *[look of concern]* What? I see . . . I see. . . . Uh huh . . . oh no, honey . . .

BEN: *[interrupting]* What's going on . . . what's wrong?

BETTY: Shush! *[waving for Ben to be quiet]*

BEN: Don't shush me—I want to know what's wrong.

BETTY: Are you sure? . . . What else did the doctor say? I'll tell your father. We'll be right over. *[She hangs up phone and begins to take off apron, looking sober.]*

BEN: Would you tell me what's going on?

BETTY: Carol just lost the baby.

BEN: What? You don't just lose a baby as far along as she was.

BETTY: *[emphatic]* Ben, she lost the baby.

BEN: Well then, what did she do wrong?

BETTY: She didn't do anything wrong.

BEN: Then what did that numbskull doctor do wrong?

BETTY: The doctor didn't do anything wrong either.

BEN: Then there's only one person to blame. *[Ben looks and points up]*

BETTY: *[fearful]* Oh, I don't know, Ben.

BEN: Oh, I do, Betty. He's messed us up before and He's done it again.

BETTY: Do you really think so?

BEN: I know who did this. . . . Who else could it be? It was . . .

BOTH: *[fists shaking upward . . .]* God!

[freeze; blackout; Music plays them off.]

8

Prayer Can Be Tough

Theme

Prayer is hard work—often we pray with the wrong motives, or we let other activities take priority. In other words, we don't, in fact, pray. This sketch points out some of the hindrances to prayer but offers no easy answers.

Characters

ETHEL: A fine Christian lady who seems to do everything right, but sometimes her prayers are for the wrong motives. She can be any age, but older works better in this sketch.

RACHEL: A fine Christian lady who also seems to do everything right, but sometimes finds excuses not to pray. Age is irrelevant.

Setting

Two identical living room sets—stage left for Ethel and stage right for Rachel—are each comprised of a chair, table, lamp, and phone.

SCENE 1

Both ladies enter at the same time and find their seat. Ready for their morning devotions, they are positive, energetic, and jump right into their morning routine. Ethel is wearing her robe, slippers, and so forth. Rachel is prim and proper, and ready for a day of luncheons and other unnecessary meetings. As one speaks, the other remains frozen.

ETHEL: *[yawns and stretches, and syrupy . . .]* Good morning, flowers and little birds, I hear you singing.

RACHEL: *[yawns and stretches, extra syrupy, appears to be looking out of a window]* Good morning, sunshine. I see you peaking through the clouds. And, Mr. Rainbow, you are so pretty this morning.

BOTH And good morning, God.

ETHEL: *[with sincere conviction]* It's time to read the Bible.

RACHEL: Yes, Lord, this is our little time together.

ETHEL: *[reading Scripture]* "The effective prayer of a godly man has great results." Well, we can just change that one word. *[looks up]* I know You won't mind. *[writes in Bible]* There . . . "The effective prayer of a godly . . . woman . . . has great results." Now I can handle that.

RACHEL: *[reading Scripture]* "Do not worry about anything, but pray about everything." Ooooo, that is so true, and I have a lot of everythings.

ETHEL: *[shows a bit of concern]* Oh, now here is a verse.

BOTH: Pray constantly.

ETHEL: Well, Lord, that's a tall order to fill, *[overly confident and very proper]* but I can handle it. And there is no better time to start than now . . . so here we go. Now, Lord, *[martyr-like]* since I have been *ever so faithful* in reading my Bible and working in *Your church* with *[begins to show some anger]* those little rug ra . . . *[catches herself, turns sweet]* "darlings" in the nursery . . . and *[turns very self-righteous]* since I was the *only one* to bring *[mean]* that complaining old Mrs. Crabfoot a meal, for which she never said "thanks" and still hasn't returned my casserole dish *[turns sweet, acting compassionate]* after her difficult surgery, *[syrupy]* I *am sure You* will do just one little thing now for me. It's about my neighbor, she needs a little help from You, God, *[turns mean]* with a holy two-by-four or something like that. . . . Not that I want any ill to come her way, but You better save her or move her to Texas, because I'm sick of her dog using my yard, and her cat enjoying my flowerbed, and her forty-seven-year-old son's junk cars are the eyesore of the neighborhood. Lord, get that boy a job or a wife. I don't care what You do with that family, just take care of them and get them out of here . . . *[syrupy again]* in your precious, sweet, and wonderful way. . . . Amen. *[momentary freeze, pause]* And don't drag Your feet. *[kindly]* Thank you.

RACHEL: *[good-natured while making her exit from stage, she looks at her watch]* Oh, my, how time flies when you're having fun . . . and, God, this is so much fun . . . but I need to run, so tah, tah, have a good day. . . . Oh how silly of me. . . . Of course You'll have a good day, after all You're God, and if anyone can have a good day, it's You. I'll see You tomorrow. I can't keep the ladies waiting. I know You would want me to be on time. We'll just have to have our little chat tomorrow. I'm sure You won't be moving and what I have is certainly no big deal to You. . . . So just take care of me and them and all the others. . . . Amen and so long for now!

[freeze and exit . . . both exit]

SCENE 2

Both women enter at the same time and find their chairs. Rachel is carrying a handbag; Ethel is carrying knitting needles and some yarn or something to sew. Rachel picks up the phone and begins to dial; Ethel begins to knit or sew. Ethel's phone rings.

ETHEL: *[picks up the phone]* Hello, . . . this is Ethel.

RACHEL: Ethel? Rachel. How are you?

ETHEL: Fine, Rachel . . . just fine. . . . What can I do for—*[looking out the window, interrupts herself as she begins to get out of her seat, sounding rather miffed]* Why you . . . little . . . Just a minute, Rachel. . . . *[puts the phone down, goes over to window, rude and loud]* Hey, you lousy dog, get out of my front yard and go to your own yard. . . . No, no, not my . . . new bush. . . . *[goes back to chair, spitting and sputtering]* Okay, Rachel, what can I do for you?

RACHEL: I just wanted to see if you could help with decorations for the annual woman's *prayer* breakfast that the church is having tomorrow?

ETHEL: Prayer breakfast? When did they start having those?

RACHEL: *[thinking as she speaks . . . staggered]* Well, it's our annual prayer breakfast . . . and this is the first annual, so we're starting tomorrow.

ETHEL: I see. . . . What are they going to do at this prayer breakfast?

RACHEL: *[reading from her brochure]* We have a wonderful quiche dish, accompanied by fresh fruit, hazelnut coffee, and Mrs. Crabfoot is making her famous blue ribbon cinnamon rolls.

ETHEL: *[with a little "bite" to it]* I hope she brings them in *my* casserole dish.

RACHEL: *[not sure how to respond]* Okay . . . We have a wonderful guest musician. Jane Adams will give a demonstration on how to do a French braid with bread dough. Then we'll have the pastor come and close in prayer.

ETHEL: Why are you calling it a prayer breakfast?

RACHEL: *[defensive]* The Reverend Kneebend is going to give our closing prayer, and I'm sure he'll mention everyone and everything in his prayer.

ETHEL: I'm not sure about all of this extra prayer stuff. *[looks out the window again]* Don't get me wrong, I think we should pray, but I'm not sure how much good it really does. Let's get real, Rachel, how has God answered your prayers?

RACHEL: *[vague and light-headed]* I pray for everyone and . . . everything, . . . and everyone and everything is doing just fine.

ETHEL: *[serious]* Rachel, be specific. What have you prayed for that you know God answered your prayer?

RACHEL: *[thinking hard, trying to speak and give an answer, but the words don't quite come out]* There was that one time . . . then there was . . . that other time . . . and several years back, no that was a coincidence. . . . *[serious]* Ethel, that's not a fair question. . . . How can I know what God is doing?

ETHEL: See, Rachel, you just made the point. Prayer is nice and good, but it's really not all that effective. *[pause]* So go ahead and sign me up to bring a quiche.

[freeze; blackout]

9

Forgiveness . . . No Way!

Theme

Forgiveness is a topic that affects everyone. But individual responses are varied and even extreme. Some don't understand what forgiveness is; some don't believe in it; others can't believe they could or should be forgiven, as we will see in these sketches.

Characters

LADY: She is ambivalent toward the idea of forgiveness. Her main point is, "I have never been forgiven."

MAN #1: The fatalist, representing the modern man who doesn't believe in forgiveness. He believes in every man for himself, and things like forgiveness are for women and children.

MAN #2: Has lived a life that is beyond any possibility of being forgiven. He has the best knowledge of what forgiveness is, but cannot believe he could or should be forgiven.

VOICE: An offstage narrator in scene 2 only.

Setting

The stage has three settings. Each character is in his or her own setting. It can be anything from a hand prop only to a full set design for each character.

Director's Note: For all characters age is irrelevant and each should be dressed in very plain attire. Black and white colors . . . any combination will be fine.

A series of three monologues and personal responses.

SCENE 1

All three enter and take a frozen position with their backs to the audience. When the light comes up on each character, that individual turns and speaks. After speaking, they go back to their original position.

LADY: *[light comes up. She turns and looks at the audience with a rather bland and cold approach—maybe even a touch of cynicism.]* Let me tell you a story. There once was a little girl who lived in a small town where everyone worked hard. She was cute, smart, and full of energy. She loved to draw and play with dolls, and she never did anything wrong. But her parents, the teacher at school, and most of her friends said she could never do anything right. After a while the little girl *believed* that she could never do anything right. So she decided to do what they wanted her to do. And she started doing everything wrong. But instead of being happy with the little girl, everyone got madder and madder and more upset with "that" little girl. Every day at school she was punished, and when she went home she was punished. Her friends made fun of her, called her names, and never invited her to play in their backyards. She never attended their parties. That little girl is not a little girl anymore. That little girl is me. I do things right, and I do things wrong—either way, it doesn't seem to matter, because I'm still punished for the right things and the wrong things. You've asked me to comment on "forgiveness." Sorry, I can't help you. You see, I've never been forgiven by anybody. I don't think forgiveness exists.

[blackout; She turns around.]

MAN #1: *[light hits, turns to audience, loose and free]* Forgiveness? Ha! What a joke. That subjective subconscious stuff is for the birds . . . women and children. Real men don't forgive! Why would they? Think about it. . . . Come on, get practical. It's a bunch of feeling stuff . . . religious talk. What good does forgiveness do? Nobody understands it. And nobody really does it. Real life goes like this, pal—you hurt me and I hurt you. Look, the Good Book says an eye for an eye and a tooth for a tooth. So what if a few of us can't see so well, and we lose a few teeth in the battle. That's life, man. That's what my old man did to me, and that's what I'm going to do with those who mess with me. So just pull up your bootstraps and move on. Have you ever had a course on, "How to Forgive"? No? Just like I thought. Now you know what I'm talking about. People say you have to forgive, but they never told you how. Face it—it's just polite, political poppycock. Forgiveness is a position of weakness. Who in their right mind wouldn't settle the score and get even. *[very forceful]* Come on, get real!

[blackout; turns back]

MAN #2: *[turns slowly with an arrogant air—as to boast of living on the edge]* Forgiveness? An absolute impossibility. With me we're talking about the unpardonable stuff. You name it, I did it. My girlfriend can't forgive me, my boss wants my head on a platter, and my own father won't even return my phone calls. Forgiveness only exists for good people. In reality, people forgive other people because it makes them feel good to forgive. You know what I'm talking about. Why do you forgive? I'll tell you why, because it's good for you . . . eases your conscience and all that stuff. If you say you'd forgive me, it's only your way of bringing up all of the garbage in my life. I go away feeling bad and you feel good. I'll cut my losses and live my life my way, and thank you very much. Later man, later.

[blackout; turns back]

Scene 2

Director's note: Scene 2 may follow immediately or sometime after scene 1.

VOICE: *[Light comes up on Lady.]* The Bible says, "In Jesus Christ, we have redemption through his blood, the forgiveness of sins."

LADY: There you go with that Bible talk. How am I supposed to understand words like *redemption* and somebody shedding blood? I told you already, no one has ever forgiven me. So how am I supposed to understand this religious talk about forgiveness? It doesn't compute. Remember the story I told you about the little girl. She only understands punishment . . . punishment for good and punishment for bad. So how am I supposed to understand anything else? I told you—forgiveness doesn't exist.

VOICE: *[Light comes up on Man.]* The Bible says, "Forgive as the Lord forgave you."

MAN #1: What we have here is "a failure to communicate." I told you this forgiveness stuff is for women and children. It's all poppycock. My dad taught me to use my fists. Now you lay some guilt trip on me because your Jesus didn't use His fists. That was His choice. He had his way, and I have mine. His way works for Him and my way works for me, thank you very much. If He wants to forgive me, that's fine. But I haven't done anything to hurt Him. *[becomes pompous]* I'm a good man and a God-fearing man. I go to church, and I pay my six percent sales tax when the plate goes by. I've never raised my fist to God, so if He has something to forgive me for, fine, but He ought to save it for those other people who are all messed up. Go preach your message to them.

VOICE: The Bible says, "If we confess our sins, he is faithful and just to forgive us our sins."

MAN #2: You see—you're just like all the rest. Now the burden falls back on me. Now I have to confess and do all the work. What did God ever do for me? This forgiveness stuff is for you, not for me. You say God forgives me. That's just a bunch of words. Do you want to make forgiveness believable? Then get my girlfriend, my boss . . . and my dad to forgive me. Yeah, there's your forgiveness challenge . . . my father. If you can get my old man to forgive me, then maybe I'll believe God can forgive me. But until then, I'm the black sheep. I'm the untouchable. What I did was unforgivable. I won't forget that, and neither should you.

VOICE: *[All three turn around.]* When you were dead in your sins, God made you alive, and He forgave us all our sins.

ALL THREE: *[look up toward God]* We wish we could believe You!

[blackout]

10

Where Are We? Heaven's Gate!

Theme

Suicide and cult followings are two topics that tend to raise questions about eternity and salvation. The reality that members face is highlighted in this sketch. This sketch is based on the real story of the Heaven's Gate cult suicides in 1997 in California, which created a lot of interest, while the media had a field day.

Characters

Bill: An everyday kind of guy and a devoted follower of Heaven's Gate Cult. He's dressed in black from head to toe.

Tom: An everyday kind of guy. Although he was in the cult, he was a doubter of Heaven's Gate teaching. He is dressed in black.

Susan: A sweet and sincere everyday kind of woman. She's from the cult's commune. She is also dressed in dark clothing.

Setting

A darkened platform, no props needed. There's just enough light to distinguish the characters.

Bill and Tom walk out onto a dark platform. Everything is slow and deliberate. Light, nondescript music could be playing in the background.

Bill: *[looking around]* Whoa, what do you think?

Tom: *[a bit fearful]* I don't know, Bill. This isn't what I expected.

Bill: *[trying]* Maybe it's just the holding room?

Tom: *[hoping to be convinced]* Yeah, that's it, some kind of waiting room.

Bill: So, Tom, what do we do now?

Tom: I was just going to ask you that.

Bill: I asked you first.

Tom: I asked you second.

Bill: All right, here's what we do. *[pause]* How about we start yelling?

Tom: *[calm and logical]* Yeah, that's a great idea. We can yell for help to get out of here or to find out where we are.

BILL/TOM: *[Both go crazy yelling various phrases.]* Help! . . . Anybody here? . . . Hello!? *[They stop together . . . pause for a moment of silence.]*

BILL: I don't think that worked.

TOM: Maybe the room is soundproof.

BILL: That's it . . . of course, why didn't I think of that?

TOM: Because I thought of it.

BILL: Whatever. *[excited]* Hey, Tom, . . . I'll bet this is some kind of psychological test . . . and we're being observed . . . by them, you know . . . and if we pass the test, they'll decide whether . . . or not to let us in.

TOM: I hope you're right, Bill, . . . this darkness and eeriness is starting to get to me just a little.

BILL: *[trying to encourage]* Maybe it's just something that we have to get used to.

TOM: *[growing agitation]* Speak for yourself. It's starting to drive me crazy.

BILL: You know this is nothing like our teacher and leader said it would be.

TOM: Boy, is that the truth. . . . You don't think he was . . . wrong.

BILL: *[jumps in]* Wrong? *[trying to be positive]* No, I think he just didn't have all of the details.

TOM: Well, he sure missed the detail on this total darkness and . . . weirdness.

BILL: You just have to hang on, Tom. Don't be so pessimistic. . . . The good stuff comes later, you know, the music, golden streets, and our mansion is just around the corner.

TOM: Look . . . maybe we should try something else. I don't care what you say, Bill, I think we've made a terrible mistake. I mean taking our own lives and catching a ride on a spaceship to heaven sounded too good to be true. And Momma said, "If something sounds too good to be true then it probably—"

SUSAN: *[walks into the darkness]* Excuse me, excuse me. Is anyone there?

BILL: *[overly confident]* See what I told you. . . . Here's our hostess now.

TOM: *[excited]* Over here. *[voice becomes fast and nervous.]* My name is Tom, and I was a faithful follower of the Heaven's Gate cult on earth. I did everything the teacher told me to, and I denied all my earthly possessions, and *[desperate]* would you please get me out of here?

SUSAN: Excuse me . . . but who are you guys . . . and could someone tell me where we are?

BILL/TOM: *[at the same time] [Bill]* A spaceship. *[Tom]* A waiting room.

BILL: Ah, wait a minute, you don't know where you are? Then who are you and how did you get here?

SUSAN: *[serious]* My name is Susan, and the last thing I remember was driving down a rainy road on my way back to the commune. I think I crashed into an oncoming car. . . . I'm just not sure . . . but I was told that after my life on earth, and, if I obeyed all the rules of the commune, then God would reward me in the life hereafter. And, well, I think I'm here, but it doesn't look too rewarding.

BILL: I guess we're all just waiting . . . here, right now, and we just have to remember all the things we were told by our teacher before coming here. We just need to believe real hard that our leader was right.

TOM: But, Bill, what if our teacher was wrong?

Bill/SUSAN: *[together]* He just can't be wrong.

TOM: *[shouts in desperation]* Then where are we? Would someone please answer?

VOICE: *[pause, silence]* Oh you wicked and worthless servants, I have thrown you into the darkness, where there will be weeping and gnashing of teeth.

[freeze; Music plays them off.]

11

Money . . . How Much Debt?

Theme

Everyone wants more stuff, and some will do anything to get it. And getting it is all that some people, in fact, think about, especially those who do not have what others have. And there are no exceptions to those who want more. Those who have much are also looking for more, but not just more stuff. This sketch reveals two neighbors who reveal their values, which are not unlike many of ours.

Characters

Bud: A real redneck. Yet, he is a believer in Jesus, even though it is hard to detect. Overalls define his casual style and manner.

Allen: A successful businessman. He has it all, plus he is very kind and very serious about his life. But he doesn't have a personal relationship with Jesus Christ. He is wearing a suit and tie.

Setting

Allen's new car—a Lexus, with a driver and passenger seat.

Both enter together from backstage as they get into Allen's car. Bud is talking as they make their way to the car.

Bud: *[loud and a bit obnoxious]* Hey, Allen, I sure appreciate the gesture. I don't often run out of gas on the freeway, but sure am glad that you came by. . . . That's what neighbors are for. *[sitting down]* Wooo wee, nice car! It must be nice making the big bucks.

Allen: *[embarrassed]* Thanks, Bud. Say, don't you go to that church on ___________? *[list a major street in town]*

Bud: Yup, the Mrs. makes me go. . . . Say, *[reaching forward to touch things]* does this have temperature control or is your clock broken?

Allen: *[kindly, but nervous]* Ah, yes, that's the temperature control, and please don't touch that knob . . . thanks. . . . *[serious]* So, do you like the minister over there at the church?

Bud: Yep, great guy. . . . Hey, what does this do? . . . *[looks up]* So that's what a moon roof is. . . . Why I never—

Allen: Bud, maybe it's a little cool to have that open. *[pause, looking for a way to approach a tender issue]* Does the minister talk much about dealing with sin and guilt . . . you know, the personal stuff?

BUD: Oh, yeah, steps on people's toes sometimes. . . . *[leans over, acting childish]* Tell me the truth, Allen, how fast will this baby go on the expressway? . . . Go ahead, *[turns around to look for police]* not a cop in sight. Show me what it will do.

ALLEN: I'd rather not, Bud, if that's okay with you.

BUD: *[teasing]* Too many tickets, huh, Allen. . . . Why you little rascal.

ALLEN: *[small laugh]* Well, there's a lot of truth to that. But does the minister offer answers to the tough questions? I mean, what do you really learn about God at the church?

BUD: Oh, ask the Mrs. She's up on all that stuff, commandments and all that. *[changing the subject]* The insurance on this must be a small fortune.

ALLEN: Well, what about the Ten Commandments? . . . Do you keep them all?

BUD: Sure do. . . . But ask the Mrs. for more details; she even has them memorized. I ought to know, she quotes them all the time. *[change up]* Wow, I love this First Corinthian leather.

ALLEN: All Ten Commandments? So you never took God's name in vain?

BUD: Not His, but maybe yours a few times. *[laughs]* Just kidding, Allen. . . . Just a little joke. . . . Tell me, how many CDs can you put in this baby? *[Bud reaches forward to test more buttons.]*

Allen Ten in the trunk . . . and please don't touch that. Come on, Bud . . . don't you lie or steal just a little . . . once in a while?

BUD: I wouldn't dare. The Mrs. would have my hide? *[leans back in pure delight]* What a chariot!

ALLEN: Does the minister ever talk about God's wrath and judgment on people who make some bad choices and mistakes?

BUD: *[serious]* Listen, if the Mrs. doesn't clobber me, God will. You don't want to mess up. *[back to the car]* Allen . . . did you keep your Cherokee or did you trade it in?

ALLEN: *[not interested]* Traded it. . . . *[shows some passion]* But isn't God loving and kind to people no matter what they've done?

BUD: *[upset]* Allen, what is it with all of the questions about church? Maybe you ought to talk to the minister.

ALLEN: I just thought you could give me a feel for how the Christian life works and how God treats people, since you go to the church every week. . . . I just thought—

BUD: I just thought that I'd be in heaven if I had a chariot like this. I'd give anything to have this car. Say, I bet the payments are huge on this baby.

ALLEN: A little stiff, Bud . . . but I feel like I owe a lot more to God than what I owe on this car. I've done a lot of stuff that I am not real proud of . . . and I was just wondering—

BUD: *[cuts him off]* Wow, . . . sounds like you're carrying a little debt with the Big Guy upstairs.

ALLEN: A lot, Bud. . . . There's no doubt I'm in debt big time, and I was wondering how to pay God back.

BUD: You better ask the Mrs. She's the accountant on all that spiritual stuff in our family.

[Light changes or music begins as both begin to talk to themselves.]

ALLEN: Well, it sure would be nice to be right with God.

BUD: Well, it sure would be nice to have a set of wheels like this.

ALLEN: I would love to give my soul to God.

BUD: I'd sell my soul to have a car like this!

[freeze; blackout]

12

Designer God

Theme

Religion is often labeled as boring and irrelevant. Therefore, people are beginning to invent their own ideas of finding, identifying, and worshiping God. This sketch reveals the process, the questions, and the concerns that many have as they consider designing their own church, religion, and God.

Characters

Jimmy: The answer man in this sketch. He tries hard to have all the "right" ideas and answers. He is self-qualified to provide humankind with the answers for religion and God. Dress is casual.

Harry: Genuinely interested in knowing God. He's tired of organized religion, yet honestly and earnestly desires to have answers to his spiritual questions. The only problem is that he will "buy in" to just about anything, especially what Jimmy has to say.

Setting

A card table with two folding chairs. Jimmy and Harry are playing a card game, Old Maid.

Director's Note: This drama can be done in two parts or one continuous sketch.

SCENE 1

Both characters are intent on the game they're playing. They're holding their cards, ready to make the "big move" as they try to bluff each other through the game.

Harry: *[conniving and teasing]* I think you are bluffing.

Jimmy: *[tough]* Harry, just play your card.

Harry: *[whining]* How come you always win at this game? It's just not fair.

Jimmy: *[arrogant]* Hey, pal, some have it and some don't. *[refers to cards]* And these little babies are the "have-its."

Harry: *[pondering over game]* Hey, Jimmy?

Jimmy: *[looking at his cards]* Yeah?

Harry: Do you and Eloise go to church on Sunday?

JIMMY: *[uninterested]* Yup!

HARRY: Do you get anything out of it?

JIMMY: Nope!

HARRY: You know, I've gone to church to meet God, and He never seems to be there.

JIMMY: Just play your card, Harry.

HARRY: *[lays down a card]* How about you, Jimmy?

JIMMY: *[annoyed]* How about me what?

HARRY: *[concern]* Do you meet God at church?

JIMMY: Look, I know you have the Old Maid and—*[pause]* No, I've never met God at church.

HARRY: So what's the point of going?

JIMMY: It keeps my wife happy. And if Eloise ain't happy, ain't nobody happy.

HARRY: *[They each play a card.]* I'm getting sick of playing this stupid game.

JIMMY: Then don't play.

HARRY: Hey, let's invent a new game.

JIMMY: *[energized]* I got a better idea, since you're into all of this church stuff today.

HARRY: *[Curious]* Yeah?

JIMMY: Yeah! Let's invent a new church.

HARRY: *[nervous]* Whoa . . . that sounds a little . . .

JIMMY: *[serious]* Harry, . . . why not? Man has created religions for the last million years. . . . It's time for a new one—one that makes sense.

HARRY: *[inquisitive]* So . . . how do we start?

JIMMY: Simple, Harry, simple. . . . *[clear and deliberate]* We just think about what we want and design a God who will get it for us. It's as easy as playing a game of cards, Harry. *[He lays down his last card.]* I win again. See, Harry . . . see how easy this is?

[freeze; blackout]

Scene 2

Jimmy shuffles and deals out cards.

HARRY: Okay, Jimmy, say we were to design our own religion. That means we need to design god. *[struggles with the idea]* So, what is he like?

JIMMY: *[comical]* Well, he's nothing like you, Harry. He's got to be someone that everyone likes . . . especially the kids . . . like a Santa Claus or a Superman . . . somebody who's always good and keeps everyone happy.

HARRY: *[buying into Jimmy's ideas]* Amen. . . . None of that policeman, judgment stuff. Makes me feel guilty. So how do we get this god to get rid of bad stuff?

JIMMY: Piece of cake, Harry. We just don't call bad stuff, bad stuff. Sin is out and "just-making-mistakes" is in. Look, we all make mistakes, so just forget about the mistakes—let time heal and move on.

HARRY: But what if I really mess up?

JIMMY: *[convincingly]* Hey, anybody can be bought, Harry. There's a price for anything. You just pay up and move on.

HARRY: *[thinking and repeats]* Pay up and move on . . . okay. . . . So how do I find this god, Jimmy? I mean what about prayer and, well, every religion has a book of rules, or a Bible, you know, a *Koran* or something . . .

JIMMY: Cyberspace . . . this is the age of Cyberspace. We just design a computer program called "God on Call," and before long everyone will believe that god is actually in the program. And the best thing is, you can turn the program on or off any time you want. Takes away all the hassle of prayer, memorizing stuff, and you don't have to chant some silly song.

HARRY: *[excited]* Wow, do I ever like that idea. *[own idea]* Then I don't have to feel . . . guilty . . . like some god in heaven is watching everything I do. Now I can just be myself.

JIMMY: You're catching on, Harry, my boy. This god, religion thing is a piece of cake. . . . Like I said, simple, man, simple. These church guys make it all too complicated.

HARRY: *[playing cards]* Jimmy . . . what about after we die?

JIMMY: What about it?

HARRY: What do we tell people about what happens to them after they die?

JIMMY: *[casual attitude]* Tell them whatever they want to hear. The good news is that no one can prove that you're wrong. . . . What better news could people get than to hear what they want to hear. It makes them feel good. And besides, people will believe anything.

HARRY: Good point, Jimmy. . . . One more question.

JIMMY: Fire away, pal!

HARRY: What happens if this doesn't work and life is still just the same?

JIMMY: Hey, don't worry so much. How can we lose?

HARRY: *[lays down last card]* Ha! I guess you have the Old Maid, Jimmy.

JIMMY: *[irritated]* Wait a minute, I never lose. I never mess up.

HARRY: *[making a subtle point]* Well, I guess you did this time! *[Both respond with a look of horror and amazement.]*

[freeze; blackout]

13

A "Little" Love

Theme

God has called us to love one another. For some that is a new idea. Too often we get caught up in loving ourselves and our stuff. This sketch reveals a little of the "little" love we "Christians" have for others.

Characters

Mr. Loveless: He's just that—stuck on himself. He's in his yard, raking leaves. A no-nonsense kind of guy, he never smiles or has any fun in life. Work, work, work is his motto.

Andy: The young neighbor boy who lives next door. His parents are just divorced, and they are experiencing some tough days.

Setting

An open stage can represent the outdoors. A rake is the only needed prop.

Mr. Loveless enters and rakes his leaves. Andy comes skipping by Loveless and stops when he hears the following line.

Loveless: *[grumbling and complaining about the weather and having to work]* I can't believe how many leaves that lousy tree produces every year.

Andy: *[Andy looks at Loveless rather curiously.]* Hi, Mr. Loveless. Were you talking to the tree? 'Cause if you were, the tree can't talk back, in case you didn't know.

Loveless: *[caught off guard]* Well, Andrew, . . . ah, I was just complimenting the tree for having such fine leaves this year.

Andy: I don't think that's what I heard. Do you and Mrs. Loveless still go to that big church with the steeple on top?

Loveless: *[trying to recover]* Ah, yes, Andy, and you and your mother should come to our church concert next Sunday.

Andy: *[rather simple]* I don't think that will be possible, Mr. Loveless.

Loveless: *[forceful]* No, Andy, you and your family need to go to church.

ANDY: I don't think we'll be able to come.

LOVELESS: *[obviously not listening]* Andy, if you're going to amount to anything, you need to find yourself in church every week.

ANDY: *[with stronger emphasis]* Hello, Mr. Loveless . . . I don't think we can make it.

LOVELESS: *[finally catches what Andy is saying]* What? What on earth for, my boy? Everyone should love to come to church. Why, we love everyone who comes to our little church.

ANDY: My dad left a few weeks ago, and I don't think he's going to come back for a long time. So I don't think we can come to church, 'cause he took the car.

LOVELESS: *[pensive]* Hmmmmmmm . . . I see. *[arrogant]* You see, Andy, that's why you need a loving church in your life.

ANDY: Mr. Loveless?

LOVELESS: Yes, Andy.

ANDY: What do you do at your church?

LOVELESS: Why . . . we sing songs, listen to sermons, and . . . pray for people.

ANDY: I've heard your singing, Mr. Loveless, and . . . I think you need to pay more attention. But have you been praying for my mom and dad?

LOVELESS: *[off guard]* Well . . . ah, yes, *[obviously not, with a voice change]* I believe that we have.

ANDY: What do you say in your prayers?

LOVELESS: *[stumped]* Ah . . . ummmm . . . that . . . God will bless all the missionaries and the people in the world.

ANDY: Are my mom and dad included with all the people in the world? 'Cause I don't think they're *[stumbles over word]* miss . . . iona . . . ries?

LOVELESS: *[relieved]* You're catching on, Andy.

ANDY: What else do you do at your church?

LOVELESS: Well, we help the poor and the homeless.

ANDY: Does that mean that your church is going to help me and my mom and my brother?

LOVELESS: Ah, well, I don't know. We'd have to run that through the committee. Might take a few months.

ANDY: I don't know how long that is, but could you and Mrs. Loveless take me and my brother to your church this week?

LOVELESS: *[phony]* Well, Andy, we'd love to, but Mrs. Loveless needs to be there early to get her class ready, and I have to be there for choir practice, but maybe we can find you a ride.

ANDY: *[catching on]* That's okay, just pretend I didn't ask, 'cause my mom doesn't want us to ride with strangers. *[pause]* Mr. Loveless, what does your pastor talk about in his sermons?

LOVELESS: *[with conviction]* Love, Andy, love and joy and commitment.

ANDY: Does that mean that you love me, Mr. Loveless?

LOVELESS: Sure, Andy, we all love you.

ANDY: Mr. Loveless?

LOVELESS: Yes, Andy.

ANDY: That's real nice, but how come I didn't know that until now?

[freeze; blackout]

14

A Story of a King

Theme

God became a man when He sent His only Son, Jesus, to this earth. In Philippians 2, we discover that truth, and the fact that Jesus gave up the splendor and glory of heaven to be like one of us and become Emmanuel, God with us. Our king in this story represents King Jesus and all that He gave up to win our love for Him, because He first loved us.

Characters

King: Dressed with an ancient crown, cape, and gold rings.

Sage: The king's advisor, dressed in first-century finery.

Fair Maiden: Dressed in a plain peasant dress, no shoes nor finery.

Narrator: One with a fine voice (can be on or off stage).

Setting

Stage right should have a throne (large chair) and a wall with a window that separates the two sets. The window can be real or imaginary. Stage left should have a simple small stool or rock with a few ferns or plants.

As narrator begins to speak, the Fair Maiden enters and sits on her stool and begins to arrange a few wildflowers she has just picked. As the narrator continues the King appears, to sit on his throne and watch the Fair Maiden out his window.

Narrator: Once upon a time there lived in a distant land a fair young maiden. She was not wealthy, she was not born to the royal throne, nor did she have abilities or talents to impress anyone. From day to day, she would come to the field near the king's palace. There, she would pick the wildflowers and bring the small bouquets to those who were poor and sick. *[King enters.]* Each day the king watched the fair maiden from the palace window, and as he did, his heart became extremely warm and affectionate for the young maiden. As his love grew, his desire to marry her became very strong.

King: *[claps his hands and sits in his chair, and with a loud voice summons his sage]* Sage! Sage! Come here at once!

Sage: *[runs to the king and bows]* Yes, Your Majesty, . . . what can I get Your Excellency?

King: Do you see that woman in my field?

SAGE: Yes, Your Lordship. She is a lovely young maiden.

KING: *[demanding]* I must have her for my wife.

SAGE: *[humble]* Yes, Your Majesty.

KING: *[instant demand]* Well, go get her for me. *[Sage is hesitant to move.]* Move along. *[forceful]* I said go get her for me.

SAGE: *[fearful]* But . . . but, sire, . . . do you want this maiden to . . . love you?

KING: Of course I do, and of course she will. . . . Now be gone with you.

SAGE: But . . . but, sire, . . . she will love you only because you are the king . . . not because you love her. She will come only out of duty and obedience as one of your subjects.

KING: *[irritated]* But, but, but . . . I don't want to hear any more, do as I say.

SAGE: Sire . . . I am afraid she will not love you.

KING: *[hesitates and actually listens with a humble tone]* Are you sure?

SAGE: I am sure.

KING: *[vold]* Then what do you suggest?

SAGE: Sire, I would suggest that you go to her and tell her you have watched her for a long time and that you have fallen in love with her.

KING: *[gets up from his throne and begins to move]* Then I will go at once.

SAGE: Excuse me, Your Lordship, but you cannot go like that.

KING: Like what?

SAGE: *[motions toward his person]* Like . . . that.

KING: *[insulted]* And just how do you propose I go?

SAGE: *[calm]* The crown has got to go, sire.

KING: *[upset]* But how will she know I am the king?

SAGE: That will come in time, Your Majesty.

KING: *[King reluctantly gives crown to sage and starts to exit.]* Wish me well.

SAGE: But you cannot go yet.

KING: *[angry]* Now what do you want?

SAGE: The cape must go.

KING: But how will she ever know that I am wealthy and of noble fame?

SAGE: That, too, will come in time . . . sire. *[He takes cape and the king begins to move out . . .]* And the rings, Your Highness?

KING: *[He takes off the rings, rather put-off, with a strong sense of indignation.]* And what is there left? I look like a . . . mere peasant.

SAGE: *[affirming]* Precisely, sire . . . and you have never looked better.

KING: *[puzzled look]* Then I am out to meet my maiden, and this better work.

SAGE: All I know is, sire, . . . she will now listen to you and believe you.

[Music plays as the king makes his way to the maiden.]

KING: Dear maiden . . . may I have a word with you?

FAIR MAIDEN: Oh, yes, sir . . . *[She extends some flowers.]* would you like some of my flowers? They are for the poor and sick.

KING: *[overtaken . . . not sure what to say or do]* I . . . don't know. . . . But . . . of course . . . I would love some of your flowers. . . . But why do you offer them to me?

FAIR MAIDEN: Because you look lonely and kind, and I see in your eyes that you have love.

KING: And that love is for you. . . . I have watched you for a long time . . . and I have a love . . . a very special love for you. *[The King takes the hand of the maiden and receives her flowers.]*

FAIR MAIDEN: I sense a sincerity in your voice, and I must bring you to meet my father and my mother in our humble home. . . . Would you come with me?

KING: Why . . . why of course I will come. . . . To be with you is my heart's desire . . . forever and forever. *[They exit; soft music plays.]*

NARRATOR: And the king and the maiden found love—true love—and in time they shared the king' palace and the lovely field where the flowers continue to grow.

[Music ends.]

15

I Had a Four

Theme

God is a spirit. No one has seen God, even though we daily see the evidence of God's existence. So Ernie and Henry are left on their own to argue the existence of a God they cannot see, and struggle with what real faith is all about.

Characters

ERNIE: Represents everyman in this sketch. He is rather confident, but places little value on spiritual things. He's dressed for the golf course carrying a #1 driver, tee, and ball.

HENRY: Ernie's good, honest friend. Henry, however, is genuinely interested in "seeing" God. He's also dressed in golf attire.

Setting

An open stage with a bench representing the ninth tee on a golf course.

Music plays as Ernie and Henry enter and walk to the ninth tee. Ernie bends over to place his ball and gets ready to tee-off.

HENRY: *[writing the scores down on a card, speaks very casually]* Are you sure you had a four on that last hole?

ERNIE: *[upset that he is being challenged, being emphatic]* Yes, I had a four. *[gets ready to swing]*

HENRY: Are you sure you counted all of your strokes when you were in the woods?

ERNIE: *[firm]* I had a four.

HENRY: *[casually]* It's amazing how you got out of the woods and onto the green in just one shot. *[Sarcastic]* You're really good, Ernie.

ERNIE: *[direct]* Yes, I am. Look, Henry, you keep your score, and I'll keep my score. Are you okay with that?

HENRY: *[writing on card]* Okay, but I think you had at least a five.

ERNIE: *[loud]* Fine, give me a five if that make you feel better.

HENRY: *[erasing and remarking]* Okay, a five it is. . . . Just want to keep you honest. That's what friends are for!

ERNIE: *[mumbling, gets ready to swing, with a very unhappy demeanor]*

HENRY: *[pensive look]* Hey, Ernie.

ERNIE: *[stops in the middle of his swing, yells, and stands, leaning on driver]* Now what is it?

HENRY: *[calm and sincere]* Have you ever seen God at that church you go to?

ERNIE: *[bitter tone]* No, I haven't seen God.

HENRY: *[curious]* Then why do you go?

ERNIE: I always go . . . and besides, Dorothy would have my hide if I didn't go.

HENRY: Then why do they call it "God's house" if He isn't there?

ERNIE: *[frustrated]* Beats me. Can't we just play golf?

HENRY: Sure, go ahead and swing.

ERNIE: *[repeats sarcastically]* "Go ahead and swing?" I've been trying to go ahead and swing, but my best friend keeps interrupting my go ahead and swing.

HENRY: *[innocent]* Oh, sorry.

ERNIE: *[cynical]* Thank you.

HENRY: *[looking off into space]* You know, I just can't figure it out.

ERNIE: *[holding club as a weapon]* Henry, do you see this club?

HENRY: Sure, what's the point?

ERNIE: It's no longer a golf club. It's a murder weapon about to kill a man on the ninth hole. *[holds club up in the air as if to strike Henry]*

HENRY: Ernie, you've been reading too many mystery novels. But since you're into mystery, how do we know God exists if you can't see Him?

ERNIE: *[irate]* How should I know that?

HENRY: Well, I just thought since you go to church and all—

ERNIE: Look, God is up there . . . somewhere.

HENRY: *[still sincerely pushing]* But how do you know?

ERNIE: *[trying to be the answer man and prove a point]* Do you know your car is in the parking lot?

HENRY: *[casually]* No, you drove.

ERNIE: *[frustrated]* Ah, fine. Do you know that your wife is home?

HENRY: *[honest and straightforward]* Nope, she went to the store.

ERNIE: *[gives up]* Look, can't we just drop this. We can't prove God exists. So just accept it by . . . faith. Yeah, by faith.

HENRY: Kind of like your golf score, huh, Ernie?

ERNIE: And what is that supposed to mean?

HENRY: Well, since I couldn't see you in the woods, I accept by faith the number of swings you made in the woods.

ERNIE: That's right, you do accept my score, and that's because we're friends, and you can trust a real friend to be honest with you and tell you the truth. Now, MY FRIEND, can we play golf?

HENRY: Sure, go ahead. *[Ernie gets ready to swing.]* Ernie!

ERNIE: *[breaks his swing again and really agitated, yells out]* What do you want?

HENRY: How do you become a friend with God?

[freeze; blackout]

16

Name That Pain

Theme

Everyone feels pain. No one enjoys pain. And no one can endure pain, unless one has learned to give their pain away to the great Healer of all pain, Jesus Christ. For those who live with pain everyday, Jesus is the answer. For those who have not met Jesus, pain is their life, as we see in this sketch.

Characters

Hugh Achers: The quiz show host. He is dressed in bright colors and is very energetic and outgoing.

Constance Payne: The chronic, out-in-the-open complainer. Dressed nicely, using a cane, she moans with every ill in medical history.

Oliver Hurtz: Defines depression and life's woes. He is dressed casually and can barely move a muscle through all the pain.

Mary Devine: Our sweet Christian who suffers pain but has learned to have victory in Jesus. She is simply dressed in slacks/sweater, and so forth.

Voice-over: Just that.

Setting

At stage right is a high table with a stool, which provides a place for our talk show host, and three stools are at stage left for the contestants. A buzzer/light system would be great, or have the contestant with the answer be the first to stand or raise a card of some kind. Two signs are utilized for the audience, reading "Applause" and "Whoa."

Upbeat music plays as contestants enter and carefully take their places. After the voice-over our host comes out and takes his place.

Voice-over: *[high/upbeat]* Ladies and gentlemen, welcome to the new game show, *Name That Pain*, where every pain is a real pain, and those who hurt are here to be honest. Please welcome our game show host, Mr. Hugh Achers. *["Applause" sign goes up to the audience.]*

Hugh: Thank you, thank you, and we're so glad you've joined us for an awful night of listening to people's pain, where pain really pays. And before we meet our guests, let me remind you that our show is sponsored by Killsall, the great pain reliever. *[holds up a huge bottle]* Now let's meet tonight's contestants. Our first guest must have been chosen by her name alone; please welcome Constance Payne. *[applause]*

CONSTANCE: *[whining]* Oh, Mr. Achers, I barely made it into the studio tonight with my arthritis and sciatic nerve problems. *[angry]* Couldn't you get lower stools? It was difficult to get up here.

HUGH: *[somewhat insensitive, yet very sincere]* Of course it is, and that's why you're here. *[moving along]* My next guest defines the word *surgery*. Would you please welcome Oliver Hurtz. *[applause]* Oliver, welcome to the show.

OLIVER: *[grumbling]* I can't believe I agreed to do this. Do you realize how much medication I had to take to come here tonight? And you'd better take those commercial breaks you promised, or it's not going to be a pretty sight up here.

HUGH: Thank you for the reminder, Mr. Hurtz. *[switching gears]* Our last guest is not a newcomer to the medical textbooks. She has had more transplants than flowers in a garden and lives in constant pain in most every area of her body. Please welcome Mary Devine. *[applause]* Mary, how are you?

MARY: *[kind, yet winces from pain]* I'm doing quite well today, Mr. Achers. Thank you for inviting me to your show.

HUGH: Thank you, Mary. Now, contestants, let me remind you and our audience that to win tonight's Hospital Package requires you to be the first to share with us your greatest pain stories by simply completing the pain-filled phrase that I give you.

OLIVER: *[loudly interrupts, looking at wristwatch]* I've got six minutes before you take the first break.

HUGH: Thank you, Oliver. Our first pain-filled phrase is "My earliest memory of pain was when . . ."

OLIVER: *[blurts out]* When I was born. I remember that doctor pulling on my head and then giving me a good whack on the backside, and it wasn't pleasant, and I'm here to tell you it really hurt. *[whoa sign]*

HUGH: Of course it did. Oliver, you receive ten points. Our next pain-filled phrase is, "The longest pain I have had is . . ."

CONSTANCE: *[yells]* My headache! I have had a mega-manic-migrane-headache for seventeen years. The pain never goes away. *[emphatic]* Never does and it never will. *[whoa sign]*

HUGH: And that's ten points for Constance. Our next pain-filled phrase begins with, "I would give anything to get rid of my . . ."

OLIVER: *[yells]* Bladder. Bladder infections all the time. Not a pretty sight. *[whoa sign]* Don't forget that commercial break. You've got four minutes.

HUGH: Thank you, Oliver, that's ten more points. Our next phrase is: "I am totally immobilized when I . . ."

CONSTANCE: *[blurts out]* Walk. Can't walk but a few inches. My toes hurt, my bunions hurt, my knees hurt, and my hip is in constant pain. *[whoa sign]*

HUGH: And another ten points for Constance. We now have a tied game—Constance with twenty points, Oliver with twenty points. And Mary with no points.

MARY: *[apologetic, yet kindly]* Sorry, I just can't top their pain-filled stories.

HUGH: Our final question is worth twenty-five points. Please complete the following pain-filled phrase. "Other than me, the person I know the best, and who has suffered the worst is . . ."

OLIVER/CONSTANCE: *[Constance and Oliver are struggling to give an answer, but cannot, and both blurt out . . .]* No one ever hurt more than me!

MARY: *[softly speaks]* Ah . . . Jesus did.

HUGH: Excuse me, Mary, did you complete our pain-filled phrase?

MARY: Oh, I guess I did. Jesus hurt more than me by carrying all of my heavy sins, and He suffered a painful death . . . for all of us.

HUGH: But, Mary, the question asks for someone that you know.

MARY: *[confident]* Oh, I know Jesus well—very well. You see, He's taken all of my pain, especially the pain of my sin. Oh yes, I know Him well. I've given Jesus all of my pain. Mr. Achers, who do you give your pain to?

[freeze; blackout; music; exit]

17 Starting Over

Theme

Everyone desires to start over, fresh and new. Our main character in this sketch discovers that starting over is not as simple as using a paper shredder. The real answer is finding new life, not trying to destroy the old life.

Characters

Ben: Represents everyman. He is dressed casually.

William: Ben's friend, also dressed casually.

Voice: Represents the voice of God offstage.

Setting

A small table, and a paper shredder is plugged in and ready for operation.

Ben enters, carrying a box, briefcase, or pile of papers that he is going to shred.

Ben: *[One at a time, he holds up a paper, names it, and shreds it.]* I'm done with you, bad dreams. *[shreds one sheet of paper]* And you're out of my life, bad report cards. *[shreds two sheets of paper]* You can take this, you lousy childhood friends. *[shreds one sheet]* And no more memories of the boss that fired me for no good reason whatsoever . . . take that, you lousy human. *[shreds one sheet]* As for you, family . . . mother . . . *[shreds one sheet]* father, . . . *[shreds one sheet]* little brother . . . *[shreds one sheet]* sister who teased me . . . *[shreds one sheet]* . . .

[William enters.]

big brother who beat me up every Saturday morning and afternoon, *[Shreds one sheet]* and grandfather. . . . *[shreds one sheet]*

William: *[overly curious]* Hey, Ben, what are you doing?

Ben: *[cordial]* Oh . . . hello, William. *[keeps shredding]* Grandmother, there will be no more hassles from you. *[shreds one sheet]*

William: *[taken aback]* Hey, what are you doing? That's your family you're shredding.

BEN: You catch on quickly.

WILLIAM: *[picks up Ben's papers, still totally curious, looks through them]* Hey, these are all of the special things out of your life's album. Why are you . . . destroying everything in your life?

BEN: Easy. . . . I'm starting a new life.

WILLIAM: *[concern]* By getting rid of everything in your past?

BEN: Why not? *[grabs papers back]* There's nothing good here, so if you don't mind, either help or get out of the way.

WILLIAM: *[irate]* But you can't just do that.

BEN: Watch me. Girlfriends . . . now I get the last word. *[shreds several sheets, one after another, calling out their names]*

WILLIAM: *[sincere]* But you loved and cared about those people.

BEN: Past tense. Susie! *[shreds one sheet]*

WILLIAM: *[dramatic]* But Susie helped you get your first job.

BEN: Jane, bye-bye. *[shreds one sheet]*

WILLIAM: Jane? Jane helped you finish your education.

BEN: So long, Betty. *[Shreds one sheet]*

WILLIAM: *[tries to grab sheet, but doesn't make it and speaks with a sense of mourning, while he watches paper go down]* Betty, you were so good for Ben. Why did you have to move away.

BEN: And now, William! *[holds up a piece of paper]*

WILLIAM: *[yells]* Wait, don't do that. . . . That's ME! You can't destroy me, too.

BEN: *[sincere]* And what have you done to really help me, pal?

WILLIAM: I . . . well, I . . . several times I . . .

BEN: *[holds paper high, ready to shred]* See you, William . . . easy come, easy—

WILLIAM: *[successfully grabs piece of paper]* No! I can't let you totally destroy your life.

BEN: My life is already destroyed. I'm just destroying the destroyers.

WILLIAM: Look, *[puts his arm around Ben]* there has to be another way than to destroy everything that's special . . . and memorable . . . and important.

BEN: Yeah? And what do you suggest, Mr. Fix-It?

WILLIAM: *[desperate]* Well, let me think. Maybe God can help!

BEN: God? *[He reaches for one more paper.]* I've got one for Him, too. See ya, God. *[shreds one sheet]*

WILLIAM: *[shocked]* Ben, now you did it. You just shredded God.

VOICE: It's okay, guys, on an old cross, my Son was shredded for you, so I understand.

WILLIAM: *[picks up all of the pieces of shredded paper that have fallen on the floor]* Look, God, Ben really didn't mean it. Here, we'll put all of these pieces back together. *[begins fumbling with strips of paper while Ben just looks on with disgust]*

VOICE: *[small laugh]* William, relax. You can't put those pieces back together. But I can. Why don't you just give them to Me?

WILLIAM: *[curious]* But this is Ben's life. How can I give you Ben's life?

VOICE: Easy. I call it prayer. Go ahead and give me the pieces.

WILLIAM: *[holds up shredded paper in a gesture of giving up pieces to God]* Okay, God, here they are.

VOICE: Thanks. Now let me take care of the rest.

[As pieces slowly fall on the ground, music plays and lights go out.]

18

Hear Ye, Hear Ye

Theme

God has instructed us to proclaim that He exists. But many other messages often get in the way, as we find in this sketch. Sometimes we need to reject the other messages and share the most important message—that God is Love.

Characters

Town Crier: Dressed in middle-ages finery.

Townsperson #1: Dressed like a peasant.

Townsperson #2: Dressed like a peasant.

Setting

An open stage is fine. No set is needed.

As music plays, the Town Crier enters, carrying a piece of parchment rolled as a scroll. The two peasants scurry right behind, anticipating some good news. English accents are appropriate.

Town Crier: *[loudly and very slowly]* La-dies . . . and gen-tle-men.

#1: *[loudly interrupting, excited, speaking to #2]* It's the ambassador for the king.

#2: *[curious and excited]* It must be awfully good news to be out on a night like tonight.

Town Crier: *[looking a bit annoyed, clears his throat, repeats himself]* Ladies and gentlemen—

#1: *[interrupts again, with concern]* Or maybe it's bad news.

#2: *[curious]* The last time he spoke it was good news, but you never know what might come out of the palace these days.

Town Crier: *[looking disgusted]* Are you about finished?

#1: *[rambling]* Yes, your royalty.

#2: We're ready to hear your good news.

TOWN CRIER: Thank you.

#1: *[humble position]* Please go ahead.

#2: *[bowing]* Yes, continue, my lord.

TOWN CRIER: *[yells]* Ladies and gentlemen, hear ye, hear ye!

#1: *[interrupts again]* My lord, please be sure to tell the good people that taxes will be reduced.

#2: *[dramatically]* Or you might tell the people there will be a great event and celebration at the palace.

TOWN CRIER: *[annoyed, a bit faster paced]* Ladies and gentlemen, hear ye, hear ye—

#1: *[interrupting]* Kind magistrate, please tell all the good people that the king is about to proclaim another holiday throughout the land.

#2: Ah, indeed another day to rest and to enjoy the bounty of our great land and kingdom.

TOWN CRIER: *[totally put out]* Hear ye, hear ye, fellow subjects and countrymen—

#1: My lord, would you be so kind to tell the people that there will be no more war with the neighboring kingdoms?

#2: And that prisoners will be given fresh bread and water.

TOWN CRIER: *[straight at the two townspeople]* Would you please stop it?! I can't announce whatever you want. I must deliver only what the king has spoken.

#1: *[critical]* Then what good are you?

#2: *[pointed]* Yeah, who needs you anyway, if you can't tell us what we want to hear?

TOWN CRIER: *[convincing]* The message from the king should always be good news to you.

#1: *[skeptical]* Well then, let us hear it.

#2: *[not enthusiastic]* Yes, try our ears.

TOWN CRIER: I would if you would be silent.

#1: Silent we are.

#2: Silent we will be. *[They begin to whisper to each other.]*

TOWN CRIER: *[confidently and loudly]* Hear ye, hear ye, fellow subjects and countrymen—

#1: *[pleading action]* I beg you, my lord, just one last request.

TOWN CRIER: *[angry]* And if this is not the last, I will order to have your head on a platter.

#1: Of course, my lord, but we were hoping that you would grant your subjects free bread . . .

#2: And cheese . . .

#1: On the fortnight of each full moon.

TOWN CRIER: *[ignores them]* Hear ye, hear ye, fellow subjects and countrymen . . . God loveth thee!

#1: I'm not sure I heard that, did you?

#2: I faintly heard something about . . . God.

#1: My Lord, please repeat the king's message.

TOWN CRIER: Hear ye, hear ye, God loveth thee. *[marches offstage]*

#1: *[beginning to walk away]* You know, the king could have done so much for us.

#2: *[depressed]* How can love, of all things, help us with our taxes, wars, and hunger.

#1: Maybe, my friend, we need to consider a new king.

#2: Indeed, one who knows what we really need.

[blackout; music; walk off]

19

Where Is This Stuff Coming From?

Theme

The voice of Satan is powerful, influencing and causing believers in Jesus to believe lies and to desire darkness rather than light. This sketch reminds us of the subtlety of Satan's voice and how easily we are deceived.

Characters

DAVE: Represents everyman, with a naive spirit and gullible curiosity. He is dressed semi-casually, wearing an apron.

JILL: Dave's wife, dressed in business attire. She's a levelheaded, clear-minded thinker, who is concerned about Dave's new way of thinking.

ENEMY: Dressed in black, representing the "dark" side. This character may be either male or female. When the Enemy speaks, Jill freezes.

Setting

A large table with at least two chairs represents a kitchen table setting or counter/work surface. Salad bowl, dressing bottles, knives, large forks, lettuce, carrots, and so forth are needed as Dave prepares a salad.

As music plays, Dave enters with an ingredient or two to begin making a salad. Dave is whistling or singing a happy tune. As he slices and dices, Enemy enters and hovers around Dave, speaking to him. Later, Jill enters. She is wearing an overcoat or jacket, which she throws on a stool or coat rack. She has just come home from work.

ENEMY: *[Music continues. From over Dave's shoulder, Enemy speaks with a critical tone.]* I can't believe you're singing a happy tune.

DAVE: *[stops, looks around as if he just heard something, ignores the reality and continues to sing or whistle]*

ENEMY: *[indicting]* Look at you! Mr. Mom? Give me a break. Your wife is out pursuing her dreams and goals, having a good time, and here you are deciding how many carrots to put in a salad.

DAVE: *[stops again, pauses to think, speaks]* Yeah, why am I stuck here making a stupid salad and not out golfing?

ENEMY: That's right. You could be out winning friends and influencing people and making the big bucks.

DAVE: *[annoyed]* Yeah, the biggest decision I make in a day is how much vinegar and oil to use.

ENEMY: Dave, you're not using your mind.

DAVE: *[slowly builds a hostile spirit, while he madly chops vegetables]* I have a great mind.

ENEMY: You're not living up to your potential.

DAVE: I have great potential.

ENEMY: You're a doormat.

DAVE: I am *not* a doormat.

ENEMY: You're wasting your life.

DAVE: *[becoming upset]* I will not waste my life.

ENEMY: You're a spineless wimp.

DAVE: *[loudly]* I am not a wimp.

JILL: *[typically tired after a long day]* Dave, I'm home. How's dinner coming? *[comes by Dave and takes a chair or stool]*

DAVE: *[very cool]* Fine, dear.

JILL: *[She dips finger in to take a taste and compliments Dave.]* Ooooooo, that tastes good. You make the best dressing.

ENEMY: She's only trying to butter you up. She's not sincere.

DAVE: *[defensive]* And why wouldn't it taste good?

JILL: *[a little curious about the negative display of emotion]* Did you have a good day?

DAVE: And why wouldn't I have a good day?

ENEMY: *[Jill freezes.]* Look what she's trying to do, Dave. She wants to compare her day with yours. Don't let her have an inch.

JILL: *[concerned]* No reason, it's just that . . . when I left the house this morning, you were in a good mood, and I just—

DAVE: *[reacts with a high level of cynicism]* Just what? Let me fill in the *what* for you. You had a great day at your office, and I had a not so great day taking care of things around the house. Is that what you mean?

JILL: *[still trying to be kind]* No, that's not what I mean. *[trying to make sense of this]* Did your parents call with bad news?

DAVE: *[becoming more upset with each comment]* No, my parents did not call.

ENEMY: Listen to her. She's trying to change the subject and blame your parents again.

DAVE: Why are you trying to change the subject, and why are you trying to blame my parents?

JILL: *[tense]* Dave, I'm not trying to blame your parents. I was just asking a question.

ENEMY: Now she's using the old question format. This is never about her. Next she's going to blame me for all of this. I've seen it before Dave.

DAVE: There you go with the questions. How come this is never about you?

JILL: Dave, if I didn't know better, I'd say there's someone else in this kitchen.

ENEMY: I told you she'd say that.

JILL: *[pulling back a bit]* This is getting a little strange.

ENEMY: You're next, Dave, old buddy. Next you're going to be called the strange one . . . or even worse. Get the jump on her.

DAVE: *[argumentative]* I suppose you think I'm strange or even stupid, and not living up to my potential. You probably think I'm just a . . . doormat or some spineless wimp.

JILL: *[rather bold]* Dave, where is this stuff coming from?

ENEMY: Well, Dave, I can't do it all for you. You're on your own. *[begins to slowly walk away]*

JILL: *[very firm]* Dave, talk to me. What's going on?

DAVE: *[rather dumbfounded]* I'm not sure, Jill, but I think I just lost my mind. *[looks at Enemy walking away]*

[freeze; Music comes up; blackout]

20

Who Are You Trying to Kid?

Theme

The second coming of Jesus Christ stirs many different emotions and expectations among believers and nonbelievers. One believer believes Jesus is coming and becomes well prepared. Another believer is skeptical. Among the unbelievers, some are interested and curious, while others have absolutely no belief in the coming of Jesus. This sketch is a metaphor of the anticipation of Christ's return.

Characters

Tom: A hard-nosed, in-your-face kind of guy. He's very logical. Dress is casual.

Melissa: She is kind and sweet. Dress is casual.

Angel: Lives on the edge, dressed in updated fashion. Colored hair would be ideal.

Billy: He is rather sarcastic, and dressed in jeans and T-shirt only.

Setting

At stage center is a table with five chairs, reflecting a coffee shop. One chair is obviously empty.

Music plays the characters onstage. Tom, Angel, and Billy come out in darkness to take a seat to drink coffee or cokes. They're in the middle of a discussion as the lights come up. After the lights are up, Melissa enters carrying two coffee cups. She places one at the empty chair and sits down, holding the other. Tom speaks.

Tom: *[in a sarcastic, angry tone]* Who are you trying to kid? Why do you do this every time we come here?

Billy: *[irritated]* Yeah, that is so embarrassing.

Angel: *[looking away]* It's weird if you ask me.

Billy: *[to Angel]* And nobody asked.

Melissa: *[sincere]* I don't care what you guys think, but He could come today and join us.

Tom: *[trying to make sense]* Look, how many times have you said that, and placed a . . . a latte there for Him and He never comes?

Billy: *[trying to be practical]* What a waste of money.

ANGEL: *[cynical]* What a waste of intelligence.

MELISSA: *[still sincere]* Fine, make fun of me. But when He walks through that door, you'll eat your words.

ANGEL: Well, it's a good thing that I'm not hungry; I could starve on a diet of my words.

BILLY: *[making a feeble effort to subdue his irritation]* Angel, pass the sugar.

ANGEL: *[sarcastic and cutting]* Get it yourself. If you would have asked nicely, I would have given it to you.

BILLY: *[sarcastic]* Oh excuse me, your royal highness. I didn't know we were so polite and formal. *[Angel rolls her eyes as Billy gets his own sugar packet.]*

TOM: Melissa, why do you believe He's coming?

ANGEL: *[negative attitude continues]* Because she's weird.

BILLY: *[mean]* Because she's going to that church down the street.

MELISSA: *[sincere and firm]* Because He said He would come.

TOM: How can you believe Him? We're not sure He's even real.

ANGEL: Yeah, how can you believe in a ghost?

BILLY: *[sing-songy]* You're dreaming the impossible dream.

TOM: Now if you told me the Antichrist was coming through that door, I'd believe you.

MELISSA: And why would you believe that?

TOM: Because this world is so messed up. What's a little more evil by one power-hungry world leader?

ANGEL: Yeah, now that makes sense.

BILLY: Well, if that six-six-six guy shows up, I'm out of here.

ANGEL: You big chicken.

BILLY: Fine, make fun, but that's one dude I'm not going to mess with.

MELISSA: *[trying to make sense of what she's hearing]* So, you guys are all telling me that you can believe in evil, but don't believe in what is good?

TOM: Yeah, that makes sense.

ANGEL: *[making fun]* Bring on the Evil One.

BILLY: *[to Angel]* You are one scary lady.

ANGEL: *[cutting]* And you are one ugly—

TOM: Cool it, you guys. I want to hear what Melissa really believes.

MELISSA: *[strong and sincere]* I really believe that Jesus is coming again. He said He would and that settles it.

ANGEL: *[challenging]* Okay, prove it.

MELISSA: *[with confidence]* Well, He came once. He promised to change my life, and three weeks ago He did. So I believe He keeps His promises.

BILLY: *[being honest]* Well . . . you are different, kind of—

ANGEL: *[jumps in]* Anybody can change for three weeks.

TOM: True, but how long is long enough to be convincing?

ANGEL: I'd give Melissa three months and she'll be "back in" with the rest of us.

BILLY: I need six months to believe she's really changed.

TOM: So, Melissa, . . . how long? *[Music chord begins and grows louder.]*

MELISSA: You can wait three or six months. But you may be sorry you waited until tomorrow.

[freeze; Entire house lights go out. Music crescendos as the cast walks off in darkness.]

21

The First Christmas Encounters

Theme

The lead character of this Christmas story is the angel Gabriel, who announces the birth of Jesus Christ to Joseph, Mary, a shepherd, and a wise man. We will see the response of each character as the angel shares the "good news." Joseph is a bit taken aback by the dream he has, even though he sleeps through most of it. Mary is first kind and positive, then rather inquisitive, but in the end she cannot wait for the day of advent. The shepherd, first fearful, isn't quite sure what to make of the whole scenario, but he'll "check it out." The Wise Man is finally in the right place at the right time. (Even though this is in a modern format, the story is primarily taken from the gospel according to Luke, chapters 1 and 2; and Matthew 1.)

Characters

GABE: A comic sort of character. He should be a wiry, happy, fun type of person. He is agent 0007. (Yes, "Get Smart" . . . Don Adams comes to mind.)

MICHAEL: Gabriel's angel friend. He's just a nice "angel" kind of guy. He's young and contemporary.

MARY: She is sweet, kind, optimistic, and outgoing—extremely inquisitive about the angelic news. With this troubling and unusual news, however, she does want some kind of credentials or proof to know that the angel is authentic (Luke 1:29). She is very young.

JOSEPH: Your everyman character. Almost any all-American, hardworking, macho-type will do. Joseph sleeps through his part; his snoring, however, and a moment of waking up indicates he actually hears what the angel has said.

SHEPHERD: A high-strung fellow. His first responses are rather macho. "Rocky" the prizefighter would be one of his folk heroes.

WISE MAN: A weary, tired fellow with strong and sincere convictions. Wearing a robe and a "Burger King" crown, he could carry a strong English accent.

NARRATOR: Just that, with a strong voice, played either on or off stage. He or she is dressed in black, maybe a tuxedo.

Setting

An open stage. A couch or cot for Joseph, one chair or stool for Mary, and a stool for the Wise Man.

Director's Note: All characters should dress in simplistic, first-century type of costumes. The angel should not be a winged creature, but wears a white turtleneck, white slacks, and black shoes.

SCENE 1: ENCOUNTER WITH GOD

GABE: *[A red phone is sitting on a pedestal down stage center. The phone is ringing. Gabe enters and answers the phone. Gabe looks at the audience, very businesslike.]* Excuse me while I answer the hotline. *[picks up phone, very articulate]* Agent Angel Gabriel, triple zero seven speaking. *[Pause, phone continues to ring, Gabe hangs up and answers his "shoe phone."]* Agent Angel Gabriel, triple zero seven speaking. Yes, Chief. Uh huh! *[looks a bit amazed]* Run that by me again, please! *[pause]* Let me see if I have this straight? You want me to tell a teenage girl that she's going to have a baby—outside of marriage—and You're calling this good news, Sir? *[pause, scrambling]* No, Sir, I am not doubting Your. . . . Yes, Chief, anything You say. *[pause]* Of course You have three more things. Chief, let me write this down. *[pulls out a small pad and pencil]* Joseph Carpenter and a shepherd must be given the same message. Do You have an address for the shepherd? *[writing and speaking]* Hillside condominiums, just outside of Bethlehem. And, yes, I'll look for a king who's riding on a camel, coming from the east side. *[skeptical]* Right, Chief, I'll see what I can do. *[new confidence]* I mean, I'll take care of it. *[pause]* And a Merry Christmas to You, too, Sir. *[hangs up phone as first song begins]*

[musical suggestion: "Lord, I Lift Your Name on High"]

SCENE 2: AN ANGELIC DIALOGUE

MICHAEL: *[Gabe enters, a bit concerned, sits on stool or edge of platform with chin resting on hands. Michael enters, reading a newspaper and carrying a trumpet or bugle.]* Hey, Gabe, did you see what *Heavenly News Today* is predicting on planet Earth? This idea for the coming of the Messiah King is going to shake up a lot of people. I wonder how the Chief is going to pull this one off.

GABE: *[Gabe just stares at Michael]* Michael, Michael, Michael, keep reading, my friend.

MICHAEL: *[mumbles a little further]* "Agent triple-oh-seven has been assigned. . . ." *[mumbles a few words, looks surprised]* You? You're doing this assignment?

GABE: *[not enthusiastic]* The chosen one!

MICHAEL: *[amazed]* Gabe, did you mess up somewhere? How in the heaven's name did you get this—

GABE: Just keep reading, trumpet player.

MICHAEL: Ohhhh . . . I see why you aren't jumping up and down. Joseph, Mary, hey, these kids look pretty young and innocent. This is going to be tough news. They could lose a lot of friends after you lay this one on them. Hey, Gabe, I'm glad this one is yours. What are you going to do?

GABE: *[holding a file folder, becomes very businesslike]* Well, this Joseph guy works third shift at his father's woodworking shop. You know, office furniture, desk units, stuff like that. He comes home about seven-thirty in the morning and takes about a four-hour nap. I thought I could catch him while he's still sleeping. And the girl, I think I'm just going to try the old honesty routine with her. Then, there's some shepherd guy outside of town. *[looking at file folder]* I don't know. The file says he's a big guy, and I might just have to *[does a sneaky move]* use a surprise approach.

MICHAEL: *[compassionately]* Gabe, have you considered a transfer to the guardian angel division? The messenger business is clearly not what it used to be.

GABE: Tempting, Michael, it's tempting. But I'm going to give this my best shot, so give me a little "Hallelujah" and I'm out of here. *[Gabe and Michael give each other a high five and freeze.]*

[music: choir or tape; option: playing the first phrase of the "Hallelujah Chorus"]

MICHAEL: Listen, I'll go punch you in! *["punch" as on a time clock] [blackout; musical introduction; Both walk off]*

[musical suggestion: "Angels We Have Heard on High"]

SCENE 3: ENCOUNTER WITH MARY

MARY: *[Soft music plays as Mary enters. She sits on a chair while doing a cross-stitch, singing a sweet simple tune, such as . . .]* "God is so good, God is so good, God is so good, He's so good to me."

NARRATOR: *[Music continues through the narrator reading Luke 1:26–28a.]* "In the sixth month, God sent the angel Gabriel *[Narrator pauses as Gabe moves out onstage into a position near Mary.]* to Nazareth, a town in Galilee, to a virgin pledged to be married to a man named Joseph, a descendant of David. The virgin's name was Mary. The angel went to her and said . . ."

GABE: *[Gabe yells at entranceway while Mary is doing her project.]* Hello! Hello! Is anybody home?

MARY: *[responds kindly but does not look up at Gabe]* Come in, the door is open.

GABE: *[formal]* Greetings, you are highly favored! The Lord is with you!

MARY: *[Mary's response is cheery and bright.]* That's a nice thing to say. *[stands]* Thank you very much. *[Gabe walks in.]*

GABE: *[hesitant]* Hi, are you the Virgin Mary?

MARY: *[embarrassed by the greeting]* That's a very personal question, but . . . yes, I am.

GABE: *[nervous]* I think you'd better sit down for this.

MARY: *[deep concern]* Has something awful happened? My parents? Joseph? Is Joey all right?

GABE: Joe . . . y is fine. . . . At least I hope he is. . . . I'm planning to go to his place next. But I think you'd better sit down, Miss.

MARY: *[bewildered]* As you say, but I can't imagine what the problem is.

GABE: *[stuttering]* Mmmmary, you yyyou are going to hhhhave a . . . a . . . a ba . . . ba . . .

MARY: *[kindly trying to help]* Go ahead, spit it out. It's all right.

GABE: Ba . . . ba . . . *[bolsters strength and with rapid fire]* baby by the Holy Spirit of God, and you will name Him Jesus, and He will be great and be called the Son of the Most High! Whew, I said it.

MARY: *[stands up, new tone of voice—tougher and bewildered]* Say what!? I don't know who you are, but you'd better leave right now or I'm going to call the—

GABE: No, wait a minute . . . I need a seat. *[moves over and sits down in her chair]* This isn't easy for me.

MARY: *[firm]* Easy for you? What about me? How in the world is this supposed to happen? By the way . . . who are you?

GABE: *[stands at attention]* I am Gabriel, Angel Agent triple-oh-seven, *[pulling out wallet]* here's my picture ID, badge, and a library card. . . . You ought to see the library we have up there, it's great. Anyway, the Chief sent me and said that He will be with you. If you have any problems, you need to call one of your relatives. *[looks at card, with amazement]* Your aunt Elizabeth at 733-7711 and she'll back me up. Oh yeah, and remember one thing: "With God nothing is impossible." Well listen, I'd love to stay and chat, but I have to go. *[looking at notepad]* By the way, do you know where I could find the Hillside condominiums near Bethlehem? *[Mary shrugs her shoulders as in not knowing. Gabe exits.]*

MARY: *[Lights dim with a spot only on Mary. Soft music plays. Seriously, she prays toward heaven.]* Father, my soul glorifies You. And my spirit rejoices in You my Savior, for You have been mindful of the humble state of Your servant. *[more intense with deep conviction]* From now on all generations will call me blessed for You, the Mighty One, have done this great thing not just for me but for all people everywhere—holy, holy is Your name!

[freeze; blackout as music crescendos]

[musical suggestion: "My Soul Does Magnify the Lord"]

SCENE 4: ENCOUNTER WITH JOSEPH

Music underscore begins as Joseph enters, sets lunch bucket down on floor, stretches out on a cot, and falls fast asleep. Narrator reads from Matthew 1:18–20a. Toward end of reading, Gabe sneaks out toward Joseph.

NARRATOR: "This is how the birth of Jesus Christ came about: His mother Mary was pledged to be married to Joseph, but before they came together, she was found to be with child through the Holy Spirit. Because Joseph her husband was a righteous man and did not want to expose her to public disgrace, he had in mind to divorce her quietly. But after he had considered this, an angel of the Lord appeared to him in a dream and said . . ."

GABE: *[music stops; leans over into Joseph's ear while he is snoring]* Joseph, hey Joe, hidy-ho there, neighbor. *[Realizing he's not going to wake up, Gabe unrolls a small scroll and reads.]* Joseph, son of David, do not be afraid to take Mary as your wife because what is conceived in her is from the Holy Spirit. *[Joseph let's out a big snort. Gabe backs off in fear, startled, looks up to heaven.]* Oh, Chief, this is not going to work. This guy is not going to buy into this idea. All right! *[continues, almost hiding behind the couch]* She will give birth to a son and you will call His name *[loud]* Jesus!

JOSEPH: *[On the word* Jesus, *he lets out a big snort and sits straight up, as if to be awake. Gabe runs away.]* Jesus!? Where in the world did that name come from? *[holding head with one hand]* I've got to quit eating late at night . . . those Mediterranean sardines with extra garlic do a number on me . . . Jesus? *[more convinced]* Jesus! Yeah I like it. *[understanding]* And Mary will have a baby right away? *[shocked]* Right away? *[hops up]* I better get down to Samuel's Club and buy a crib.

[exit, blackout]

[musical suggestion: "God Will Make a Way"]

SCENE 5: ENCOUNTER WITH A SHEPHERD

Music underscore is played—ideally a flute with a pastoral theme. As soon as the Scripture reading begins, the shepherd comes out and leans on his shepherd's staff.

NARRATOR: *[Luke 2:8–9]* "And there were shepherds living out in the fields nearby, keeping watch over their flocks at night. An angel of the Lord appeared to them, *[Gabe sneaks up on the shepherd.]* and the glory of the Lord shone around them, and they were terrified." *[Shepherd is frozen, standing asleep. Gabe taps the shepherd on the shoulder. It scares the shepherd into a yell.]*

SHEPHERD: *[towers over Gabe, intimidating him]* Hey, pal, who do you think you are sneaking up on a perfect stranger? *[grabbing Gabe's shirt and pointing into his chest]* I hope you have a good answer. Are you trying to steal my sheep?

GABE: *[scared]* No, Mr. Shepherd, I'm not a rustler. And, sir, it has taken me nine months to find you. But I have a telegram. Could I read it please? *[reading from telegram]* To Mr. Shepherd, from God, stop. Do not be afraid, stop. I bring you good news of great joy that will be for all the people, stop. *[Gabe keeps looking to check on the shepherd's responses.]* Today in the town of David a Savior has been born to you; he is Christ the Lord, stop. This will be a sign to you: You will find a baby wrapped in cloths and lying in a manger, stop, end. And, hey, listen don't worry about a tip, this one is on me, okay? . . . and have a nice day.

SHEPHERD: Let me see that thing. *[Shepherd grabs Gabe and telegram, mumbles as he is reading it.]* How do I know this is legit?

GABE: *[confident]* Well, sir, how about checking it out for yourself?

SHEPHERD: All right, my flighty little friend, but you're coming with me and the boys, and you better be right. *[Grabs Gabe as they exit. "Theme from Rocky" could be played. Lights fadeout.]*

[musical suggestion: "O Holy Night"]

SCENE 6: ENCOUNTER WITH A WISE MAN

NARRATOR: *[Music underscore. During reading from Matthew 2:1–2, the Wise Man hobbles onstage and sits on a stool and rubs his feet.]* "After Jesus was born in Bethlehem in Judea, during the time of King Herod, Magi from the east came to Jerusalem and asked, 'Where is the one who has been born king of the Jews? We saw his star in the east and have come to worship him.'"

WISE MAN: *[music fades]* Oh my aching feet. *[looks up through a pair of binoculars, with a tired and weary voice]* Now, where is that star? Two years—and I'm still following a star. I can't believe I signed up for this.

GABE: *[Gabe enters the scene during the Wise Man's first comments.]* Excuse me, sir, I couldn't help but overhear your dilemma. You're looking for a star, and I believe I can help you.

WISE MAN: Oh goodie, another wise guy. Look, pal, I have two other guys who insist on following me around; by the way, hand me some of that oil o'frankincense in my bag, would ya?

GABE: Absolutely. *[finds a bottle of lotion and hands it to him]* And, yes, I know you are one of the three wise men.

WISE MAN: Great, now everyone knows we're coming. Herod is going to have our heads—so much for a covert operation. And I don't know how wise we are. Do you realize the price of camel fuel these days? When I go back East, I'm having a word with the OPEC people.

GABE: Well, Mr. Wise, would you like the directions to the new King?

WISE MAN: *[exhausted]* Sure, kid, I'm open to just about anything. You know, I think we took a wrong turn somewhere around the Dead Sea—and this sand has done a number on my blisters. So fire away, pal.

GABE: You want to go straight up past Jericho, take a left at the Sea of Galilee, up over two ridges, and there's a small town called Nazareth. The boys and I put the star right over the carpenter's shop. You can't miss it. See ya.

WISE MAN: See ya? *[yells out]* Hey, wait a minute, who are you? *[takes out a small coin purse]* Here, let me give you something for the directions?

GABE: *[positive]* Just give everything—and I mean everything—to the baby King. You'll be glad you did.

WISE MAN: *[with a sense of wonder]* Give everything to the King? Now how did he know that?

[freeze; music interlude; blackout]

[musical suggestion: "We Three Kings"]

SCENE 7: FINAL ENCOUNTER WITH GOD

At the beginning of this section, audience could be led to sing "Joy to the World." During an interlude before the last verse is sung, lights dim, and the red phone is put in place. The phone rings and Gabe enters. Gabe goes through the same routine as in the beginning, and ends up picking up his shoe phone.

GABE: *[articulate]* Agent Angel Gabriel, triple-oh-seven speaking. *[pause]* Yes, Chief. Yes, I do have a report. *[embarrassed]* Yes, Sir, I know it's been a few years. *[enthused]* But, Chief, You won't be disappointed. Everything has worked out just the way You said it would. *[pause]* Of course You're not surprised, and yes, I will get on with it. The facts are simple, Chief. Everyone loves Your Son, and they are beginning to follow Him all over the world. And, Sir, if I might add, He's amazing—"awesome" is what some are saying. You wouldn't believe the miracles He is doing. *[pause]* Everywhere I go, I see Jesus preaching the Good News. And, Sir, lives are being changed. There are a few who don't get it yet, but I know You'll take care of all of that. So, thank You, Chief, for all that You've done. *[Pause, music for "Joy to the World" begins to crescendo.]* And Merry Christmas to You, too! *[Gabe may freeze, or exit, or join in the singing of "Joy to the World."]*

[Audience is led in completing the song "Joy to the World."]